PERGOLAS
ARBOURS·GAZEBOS
FOLLIES

PERGOLAS
ARBOURS·GAZEBOS
FOLLIES

DAVID STEVENS

WARD LOCK LIMITED · LONDON

© Ward Lock Ltd 1987

First published in Great Britain in 1987
by Ward Lock Limited, 8 Clifford Street
London W1X 1RB, an Egmont Company

House editor Denis Ingram
Text set in Caledonia
by MS Filmsetting Limited, Frome, Somerset

Printed and bound in Spain
by Graficas Reunidas

British Library Cataloguing in Publication Data
Stevens, David, *1943–*
   Pergolas, arbours, gazebos and follies.
   1. Gardens——Design 2. Garden structures
   I. Title
   717   SB472

   ISBN 0-7063-6555-0

Contents

Preface

Simplicity is the key to good design and nowhere is this more apparent than in the garden. The problem with such a basic rule is how to relate it to an inherently complicated subject, a subject that is full of ever changing patterns that rely on the turning seasons, the vagaries of the climate and not least the gardener's own personality.

It is of course the last that holds the key to any composition. It is here that the basic garden components are resolved; room to sit, paths for access, buildings for storage or greenhouses for growing, lawns, trees, plants and vegetables. All of these will be honed into a particular pattern, reflecting an individual character and underlining the point that no two plots can ever be identical. While such components are the backbone of a design it is planting and ornamentation that really brings things together. No garden is complete without these, but the prime consideration, particularly with the latter, is their utilization in a sensible, coherent and not least elegant manner. A surfeit of focal points is not only restless but boring. Good design is quite the opposite, relying on positive statements allied to a degree of surprise that can lead both feet and eye through what is essentially an outdoor room, in a most delightful way.

The scope of this book is to look at what are essentially the larger ornamental structures within the garden framework. In fact, as far as pergolas are concerned, they may well provide all or part of that framework. It is also true that there is nothing new in gardening and from the very earliest times arches and overhead beams have been vital for the training of vines and other plants to provide both food and shelter from a powerful sun. In so doing they naturally spanned paths and provided division, becoming essential parts of the garden plan.

Equally it could be argued that man's earliest dwellings were within caves, a subject returned to with considerable enthusiasm in the great landscape parks of the eighteenth century. Then grottoes were something of a passion for gentlemen with extravagant tastes, financial obesity and a sense of humour to match. You might be forgiven for thinking that such whims were the preserve of a bygone era but not so. A particularly charming client of mine had me construct a grotto within his grounds, complete with hired hermit who, clothed in a tailor-made robe of hessian, would, for a substantial retainer, regale astonished guests with quotes from *Paradise Lost*.

Gazebos on the other hand are far from impractical. They are quite simply rooms with a view, so their location is of paramount importance. Again they have historical significance and their history runs roughly parallel with follies. Such delightful little buildings were strategically placed to look in or out of a garden and over the years their kin has come down to us in the form of summer-houses, which should always be free standing and never tacked on to a building in the form of a conservatory.

So whether it be folly, gazebo, pergola or arch, history has taken a firm hand in their development. Today's problem, however, is not so much how to recreate these visual delights, but how to remove them from their grand ancestral setting and find a place for them in the altogether more constricted confines of a modern garden. This is far from easy as commercial pressures have in many instances reduced all of them to a travesty of their former glory. Follies became pixie cottages, gazebos ridiculous alpine summer-houses, while pergolas and arches can be seen in a thousand garden centres as tortured extrusions of plastic-coated wire. The mighty have indeed fallen, but thankfully not without a degree of hope. The basic concept of all these remains alive and well, and continues to be constructed by professional garden architects and gifted amateurs up and down the country.

Another joy is that they have all become a thoroughly indigenous part of the English garden scene. It is true that you can see likenesses all over the world, but for my money a lazy arbour decorated in high summer with hollyhocks and climbing roses, or a starkly realistic ruin looming out of a Hampshire mist, have a ring of truth that refreshes me whenever I return from working overseas. My own enthusiasm for the subject stems from a formal training in landscape architecture and an increasingly varied career spanning more than fifteen years. Throughout this time one slowly gains an insight not only of the vast range of styles and idiosyncrasies that have been built, but also the way in which they can be used in a contemporary setting.

English garden design is in a state of flux, sweeping away many of the fussy conventions beloved by the Victorians. In many ways it is returning to the simplicity of those great landscape parks, albeit on a smaller scale and altogether different criteria. Such change has already profoundly affected both the American and Scandinavian approach to living outside. Theirs is an uncluttered and, some would say, clinical style. In this country we are moving in the same direction but the end results are neither so austere nor so simple. The English are by nature individualistic in their approach to gardening and, almost certainly, always retain a fondness for ornamentation in all its guises.

Whether your interest is historical or contemporary, the content of this book is fascinating. In many ways the subject is also unusual, and as someone engaged in the landscape design profession, I learnt a great deal during its preparation. This fact alone convinces me that follies, gazebos, pergolas and arches have an increasingly important role to play in the garden. Look at the options, refrain from slavish mimicry and produce something that reflects your own personality; the result will delight you.

D.S.

1

Design Considerations

THE IMPORTANCE OF PLANNING

I always find it rather odd that although most people are quite capable of planning the inside of their homes, the outside seems to get forgotten. Not always, to be sure, for there are some delightful examples of good design where house and garden are treated as a single entity, the one flowing on and out from the other. Why some people should be better at this than their neighbours has little to do with formal training, or even botanical knowledge. The worst culprits are often architects and for the life of me I can never understand how the rhythm and obvious competence of a good working drawing can degenerate into a meaningless jumble of unrelated features outside the confines of four walls.

Garden planning relies heavily on commonsense, as does all good design, and there is absolutely no credence in the belief that designers conjure inspiration from thin air. Any architect, landscape or otherwise, works from a set of well tested rules that he or she knows will generate a degree of success, although this should never preclude original thinking and genuine inspiration which is often born of experience. Such talent can lift one from straightforward ability into an altogether far higher plane. From my own point of view I always strive for excellence and am usually satisfied with the end product, after more or less work. There is no doubt however that on occasion things come together in a different way that makes me glow with enthusiasm in the certain knowledge that there is something more involved than plain competence.

Hypothetical self-congratulation is all very well but what we really want to know is how to plan our garden in basic terms and, more importantly, locate the features that are the subject of this book. To do this an understanding of a few basic design rules is essential.

The trouble with most of us is that we are governed by impulse rather than anything else and this means that on the first fine day in spring we rush to the nearest garden centre, buy a bootful of paving, pots, plants and assorted goodies and subsequently arrange these in some state of disarray in the garden. Such outings more often than not happen at irregular intervals throughout the year and produce results that, while perhaps pleasing, lack any real purpose and almost certainly fail to realize the full potential of your 'outdoor room'. Focal points and features are of course an integral part of all this, but by their very nature they need careful siting and cannot be just slapped down anywhere. If they are, the picture is confused and they lose their inherent strength.

Perhaps one of the most important elements of garden planning is therefore patience, or at least a degree of restraint.

Having run a landscape planning service for a national magazine for many years, I have evolved a straightforward questionnaire that allows all relevant information to be put together on a single sheet of paper. It is divided into two sections and asks quite simply 'what have you got?', and 'what do you want?'.

WHAT HAVE YOU GOT?

This question involves a very basic survey to check the overall dimensions of the plot, any changes of level, the direction of prevailing winds, position of existing features that might include trees and planting, types of boundary fencing, etc. It should also include the north point (or where the sun shines at midday), the possibility of good or, more likely, bad views and any other factors both within or outside the garden that might impinge on the layout.

Without going into the technicalities of surveying, be sure to use a long tape and take this from one side and then one end to the other, jotting down 'running' measurements as you go. Never try to measure from point to point in isolation, the outcome can be most confusing! A very simple survey takes all these factors into account, and when this is converted into a scale drawing on graph paper it will not only form the basis for an accurate design but will obviate the dangerous practice of creating compositions on the back of envelopes, a sure recipe for disaster. Such a survey applies equally well to a brand new plot or an established garden that may well need modification and, where the latter is concerned, be sure to indicate all planting however unpromising this may seem.

As an indication of how important this is, I was working on a garden recently that was straddled by an ancient and unkempt blackthorn hedge. The owners were convinced that this should go, it being part of an older garden that had been divided into building plots. With careful thinning and pruning however, I managed to work it into the new design so successfully that it became not only a natural division but also a frame for a newly created view beyond. This was living sculpture, a screen, pergola and arch all rolled into one and what's more it was free! It could have served equally well as a backdrop for any kind of building, including a gazebo or even, at a pinch, a quaint but not impractical frame for a folly.

At this stage, however, one is not even considering such ideas. These come much later on, and certainly not before the survey has been transferred to a scale drawing. To do this, take a sheet of graph paper and use a simple measurement of, say, one square per foot, or five squares per metre. Mark in all those things shown on the survey and when you have finished take one or two photocopies

that act as an insurance against losing the original. Our survey has been transferred to a scale drawing as shown in Fig. 1. You can see that it is a very average plot measuring 33.5 m × 9 m (110 ft × 30 ft). It has an awkward apex at the top, a number of old fruit trees and is uncompromisingly flat. It has the advantage of facing south but is typical of thousands of contemporaries that we pass on the train when entering any large city.

WHAT DO YOU WANT?

Such a garden, apart from having to fulfil the normal functions of a terrace for sitting and dining, can incorporate any number of personal requirements. These might include barbecues, pools, sandpits, vegetables, lawn, planting and many other items. Not only do any or all of these have to fit in somewhere, but they have to blend into an overall composition that provides a feeling of space and movement, detracting from boundaries that are almost inevitably rectangular.

In our situation we have chosen to illustrate the importance of a series of focal points that lead one down the garden creating 'pools' of interest. It also proves the point that although under normal circumstances one would not consider using *all* the subjects of this book, it can not only be achieved but also brought about in such a way as to provide a fascinating perspective.

Moving away from the house, the paved area is of ample size and utilizes a combination of neat precast slabs and brick, the latter helping to soften the overall surface as well as providing a visual link with the adjoining building. The paving pattern is designed to lead the eye diagonally across the space, opening up the latter and tying the built-in seat into the overall composition. On the other side of the terrace the raised bed and herbs echo the interlocking brick rectangles, the low aromatic plants being framed by an equally fragrant clipped lavender hedge. Lin-

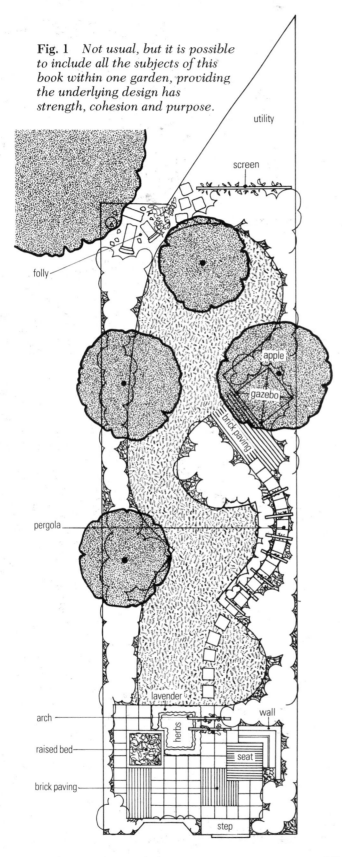

Fig. 1 Not usual, but it is possible to include all the subjects of this book within one garden, providing the underlying design has strength, cohesion and purpose.

king the two sides of the terrace and acting as both a gateway and frame to the garden beyond is the first of our garden features, a simple archway smothered with a perfumed honeysuckle. In isolation the arch would not be effective, but reinforced as it is by the combination of planting, seat and raised bed it forms a focus and 'tension point' that leads both feet and eye in a preconceived direction.

With what is essentially a long narrow garden we need to emphasize the inherent width of the plot at the expense of the length and, to do this, the path that leads on from the arch swings away to the right-hand side in a gentle curve. Another task, and another essential component of any good garden design, is to create a feeling of mystery, preventing the overall concept from being seen in its entirety from any single viewpoint. In order to reinforce this, our path slides away softly under a pergola, from light to dappled shade, and continues on its way with a series of fragmented views that increase the visual space and encourage one on towards the end of the tunnel and the next 'outdoor room'.

A gazebo is quite simply a room with a view. It is not a summer-house, shed, conservatory or battered lean-to that may be tacked onto the rear of a house as an afterthought to satisfy a family whim. It serves a visual pleasure and in our garden acts as a punctuation mark at the end of the path and pergola. Such a feature – any feature for that matter – must have a positive place to go. A surfeit of focal points is restless, a dearth is boring. In this design the building sits comfortably to one side, roughly equidistant between the terrace and bottom boundary. It has been positioned carefully to be viewed from and have a view back towards the house. By being to one side rather than in the middle of the space it sets up a diagonal axis and this creates a feeling of greater space, a diagonal line always being the longest across any

This eccentric house extension is a genuine attempt to produce a restless and bizarre end result – in the best tradition of contemporary follies.

rectangle. The old apple tree acts as a backdrop and any garden building benefits from the softening influence of branches and planting that enhance rather than detract from an architectural line. Brick paving forms an informal sitting area, indicating a change of use from the precast slabs that form the path.

This area really is the main pivot of the garden: towards the house lies formality, away in the other direction things become altogether less rigid. Here the lawn and border shapes are built up from strong flowing curves that provide that necessary feeling of continuity. As a final statement of eccentricity a simple folly crumbles its way from the far corner of the garden, flanked by old brick walls. Follies need not be grand and in a domestic situation are better off being unobtrusive. Humorous certainly, a patina of age essential, but little more is needed or asked for. Here three old stone columns have been placed carefully as though they have fallen into the shrubbery a long while ago. Plants and climbers have entwined around the stonework, and these in turn scramble over the final archway and screen that hides the practical utility area right at the bottom of the garden. The folly is rightly isolated in that corner. A path to it would be quite wrong and far too obvious. Its charm lies mainly in the fact that it should be 'happened' upon, glimpsed from the gazebo by the casual observer.

In this garden all the features are unashamedly gathered. None of them clash and this is due largely to the configuration of the plot. Long narrow gardens are always ripe for subdivision and you can move from 'room' to 'room', each having a separate theme or main attraction. By using this technique one again creates a feeling of greater space, continuity being provided by the lawn and planting. Perhaps the greatest lesson to learn is the provision of continuity, one element flowing on and out from another. In essence the more features there are the more difficult this becomes and it is in this area that the designer's skill is paramount.

SQUARE GARDENS

Square gardens are quite different and small square suburban gardens are perhaps the most difficult of all. Where the long garden has inherent movement, much like a tall man in a pinstripe suit, the square garden is completely static. One solution is to turn the whole design at an angle of say 45° to the house and boundaries, setting up a pattern of more interesting diagonals. Another is to look for interest within the plot, turning the design in upon itself to detract from barren fences and a hostile city environment. Remember too, where space is limited budgets can often be utilized more effectively; after all, a given sum for a large garden can get diluted to the point of insignificance, but that same amount of cash provides ample scope in a courtyard.

Another problem in the town is, quite simply, proximity to neighbours. They can see you, and you can see them along with the buildings they occupy. In such a situation the answer may lie in the use of beams and all kinds of overhead structures, which while not always obscuring a view can at least soften what are, after all, alien surroundings.

In the little garden shown in Fig. 2 the brief was, for ease of maintenance, room to sit, an envelope of colour and, if not total privacy, at least a degree of intimacy. As well as this, access to the back gate would need to be maintained and there was a special request for a small lawn. The latter is not always practical in a tiny garden, but in the absence of dogs and children it can be delightful, bringing an unexpected breath of rural air to a claustrophobic situation.

A preference for traditional materials set the theme and a generous paved area in rectangular old Yorkstone was softened by panels of granite setts. The latter are cube or brick-shaped and can be fitted neatly into areas between slabs that would otherwise necessitate the laborious task of 'cutting in' hand-finished stones.

Instead of subdividing the garden into

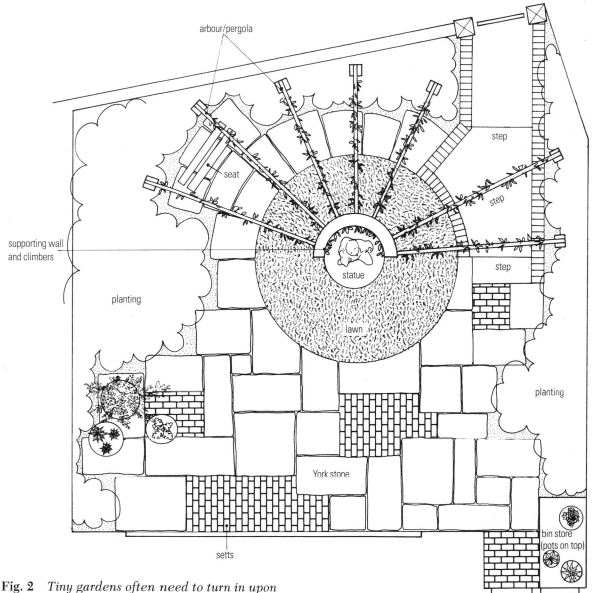

arbour/pergola

step

step

step

seat

supporting wall
and climbers

statue

planting

lawn

planting

York stone

bin store
(pots on top)

setts

Fig. 2 *Tiny gardens often need to turn in upon themselves, leading the eye away from awkward boundaries and uncompromising views. Here a small lawn is flanked by a generous terrace, the pergola screening views from adjoining properties.*

separate areas the terrace sweeps around the circular lawn, becoming both a path and feature in its own right. The steps drop away comfortably at one point, the path continuing, bringing one gently round to the arbour. An arbour is something of a hybrid: a cross between arch, pergola and overhead beams. It should form a canopy onto which climbing plants can scramble, and if these are fragrant then so much the better.

In this case the arbour is part of a larger composition that forms the central pivot and main focal point of the garden. This is a circular pergola, starting at one side of the terrace to avoid shadows on the sitting area. The pivot of the beams is a circular bed and stone slab in the centre of the lawn. Within this is placed a well chosen statue that will provide interest throughout the year. The pergola thus spans both lawn and path, merging to become part of the arbour. Such a design tends inevitably to look raw when first constructed, but when planting becomes established it takes us into the third dimension in a most attractive way. It also has the advantage of providing a really effective screen through well over 180° of the garden, particularly from the upstairs windows of houses opposite. Perhaps the most important factor in using all these garden features is to remember that they act as the 'bones' of the garden. As such they form but half the end product. The bigger the structure the more dominant they appear, and there is always a school of thought that embraces the 'brash is beautiful' syndrome. This is quite positively *not* what good design is about and any feature should be so positioned as to be not only subtle but to blend into a backdrop of planting that also retains colour and interest throughout the year.

PLANTING DESIGN

In fact, planting to most people *is* gardening and once the framework of hard landscape features has been set it is time to bring the whole composition to life. As with the basic design, over-complication spells disaster and the garden that is filled with a myriad different species quickly becomes restless. Plants should therefore reinforce the basic pattern, leading the eye through curves and angles as well as creating depth and mystery. Apart from these purely aesthetic considerations there are the practical aspects of wind, shelter, screening from a bad view or the enhancement of a good one.

In order to fulfil all these functions the planting plan or sequence should be broken down into two distinct stages. First comes the implementation of a framework of larger, stronger and in all probability evergreen plants that can form a background against which the more delicate, colourful material can later be interwoven. In natural woodland there is a similar classification, trees forming the highest canopy with shrubs below, followed by a scrambling ground cover that forms a thick carpet.

We have already seen that trees can add immeasurably to a garden, providing both vertical emphasis and sufficient scale to balance the visual weight of a decorative building. Not only can they be positioned behind or to one side of a structure but they can be set some distance away as a natural counterpoint. Moving down the scale shrubs and the larger herbaceous plants take the eye lower. Here one is looking for not only scale but a definite line that might be vertical, horizontal, round or flat. The possibilities of such planting close to a building are enormous. The tall graceful line of bamboo beside a folly, a stunning mature purple Japanese maple arching towards a white gazebo or the festoons of Laburnum blossom tumbling through a metal pergola all have a mystical quality that can go a long way to make a particular situation memorable.

As well as providing height and cover a degree of fast maturity is also important, so interplant with faster growing species such as buddleia, broom or dogwood to get things moving as soon as possible. Many such plants are relatively short-lived and can therefore be removed as the slower species mature, knitting together to form a permanent framework.

Think how these points would enhance our initial design, structural plants really holding the overall composition together. Against these the more intricate species can be given full rein, and, where the 'skeleton' shrubs are grouped in threes and fours, the latter can be used in drifts of five to ten, or even more.

But all this supposes a picture in monochrome and the final breath of life is colour. Gertrude Jekyll, a plantswoman of real sensitivity from the early part of this century, has left us a legacy of writing and a number of restored gardens that have increasingly raised our awareness of planting design. Not only did she have a deep understanding of the juxtaposition of species with regard to form and difference in texture, she also had a painter's ability to use colour.

COLOUR

In very basic terms this emphasized the importance of using flowers in colour ranges that placed the hot red, yellow and orange in one band, the cool blue, pink, purple and white in another. Grey, that great harmonizer in any design field, acts as a link and softening influence.

Hot colours draw the eye and if placed at any distance from a viewpoint foreshorten a space. A tub of bright red salvias placed at the far end of our long narrow garden would rivet attention at the expense of all else. Of course, this is entirely counterproductive and would defeat the object of the features and gazebo that we so carefully positioned.

If used properly, colour can increase a feeling of space to this group, the more vibrant hues closer to the house or viewpoint, allowing the softer pastel shades to drift away towards the bottom boundary. A dashing red rose on the archway framing the terrace would be delightful leading into a cascade of wisteria over the pergola. In between lies a rich diversity of planting that relies heavily on form and foliage and this in itself does much to complement the architectural line of such strong vertical structures. The gazebo in the middle distance is a simple timber building and here the ideal foil is white. For flower interest, you could include lilies, the climbing rose 'Swan Lake', and those delightful dog daisies that flower all summer long. Foliage too adds to the picture with the invaluable leaves of *Philadelphus coronarius* 'Variegata' adding height as a tall shrub, echoed at ground level by *Hosta* 'Albopicta'.

Of course purist planting always runs the risk of verging on blandness and it is here that the subtle introduction of a dash of colour can work miracles. My own favourite against white is that stunning little orange herbaceous plant, *Geum × borisii* – but not alone, let it work against a fragrant buffer of green tobacco plants, *Nicotiana alata* 'Lime Green'. Invariably the effect is quite stunning.

As a final planting statement the folly needs not only mystery, but a patina of age. Being the most distant feature it should be undemonstrative and here we can use all those species so beloved by the Victorians in their gothic flights of fancy: Aucuba, bamboo, Castor oil plants and, above all, ferns. Ferns that can nestle in stone crevices, arch over the fallen columns, and droop with melancholy from the old wall behind. Our folly is in deep shade, tucked in the angle of that north-facing wall. All plants mentioned above thrive in such positions and every one, apart from the ferns, is evergreen, providing both interest and a degree of drama throughout the year with bold foliage patterns, even on the shortest, darkest winter's day.

If one is to learn a simple lesson from good garden design, and how garden features may be used to produce harmony, rather than suburban clutter, then one should appreciate that the composition is a total entity and not a series of unrelated weekend whims. Take your time in the planning, work out what you want and, perhaps most important, what you dislike. Above all use discretion. Remember, a garden is more than a passing passion and is quite capable of surviving several lifetimes. Not only is it a living, growing thing, it is also a part and reflection of your own personality. If you have a fondness for the subjects of this book, choose and position them with care. If you undertake that, then the rest will fall into place quite naturally.

2

Arbours and Overheads

The dictionary definition of arbour simply states, 'Bower, shady retreat with sides and roof covered with climbing plants'. It describes a deliciously English picture of high summer where, in the far corner of a garden one can happen upon an informal structure of overhead beams that cast dappled shade on a sitting area below. Such creations are timeless, and my first memories of our own garden in Devon are of just such a place. To a small boy there was an element of mystery too, the roof of rustic timbers seemed higher and stouter, the giant spires of hollyhocks needed an upward glance and the profusion of fuchsia buds provided endless fun as one 'popped' them to reveal the flowers within.

Because the place was slightly derelict it became a den, castle and retreat rolled into one. Hours were spent reading or drawing, friends would come for alfresco picnics and, from time to time, to illicit midnight feasts. All this in the arbour which made it, unwittingly, the very fabric of a garden. After all, the highest acclaim of any feature is that it is well used and loved, by children as well as adults.

HISTORY

In historical terms, the arbour is far from English and can claim a long pedigree back across Europe and the Mediterranean, to the home of civilization on the Nile Delta. In fact, cultivation of the grape vine, which begins this story, undoubtedly reaches much further back in time, and in all probability well over 10 000 years ago. Then up to 6000 BC, wild grapes were used to produce a crude wine in the areas occupied by Armenia. Slowly hybridization took place, the strains improved and the first recorded vineyards appeared in

Mesopotamia. From there it was a short step to Egypt. Here we have some fascinating wall paintings depicting vines grown over a variety of structures, all of which could loosely be termed arbours. At this point in time, something over 4000 years ago, arbours were productive rather than decorative features, their shapes ranging from tunnel-like supports, inevitably constructed from timber, to those that were round, where the stems themselves provided the frame. Although they were functional, it must have become obvious that here was a perfect retreat from an environment dominated by bright light and a torrid sun. A living framework of stems allowed one to take advantage of any breeze far more than a solid building.

In fact it would not be difficult to recreate the rounded pattern and this could form a delightful spot in any domestic garden at minimum expense. Why not experiment with some iron hoops set in a circle, the top of which would need to be some 2 m or 2.5 m (7 ft or 8 ft) high? Attach chicken wire around leaving a gap through which to enter, and carry this right over the top to form a canopy. Plant and train virtually any climber on to the structure and you have what could be described as a vegetative igloo. A more sophisticated and expensive solution would be to use sections of rectangular mild steel or wrought iron. These could be hooped in a similar way as described and drilled at regular intervals to accept galvanized wire. This was not uncommon during Victorian times. I have seen an example, rather the worse for wear, carrying a wisteria, whose branches, thick with age, had distorted the iron into an almost unrecognizable shape.

In the historical context the arbour moved on, still as a vehicle for vines, to Crete, Greece and finally Italy where the Romans with their genuine love of outdoor living let their imaginations take flight with a wealth of designs. The records of these are numerous and illustrate the Roman fascination for regular pattern and bold, if mundane, architecture. Many arbours were supported by stone columns, some of which were even topped with busts or heads of animals. Most had open lattice roofs and squared timber, although others show curved wooden vaulting of considerable grandeur. My own view is that the Romans, in design terms, tended towards vulgarity; they were a dominating race and this showed in their heavy-handed approach to virtually everything they undertook. Unfortunately, there is a similar style of suburban gardening today, and the market is swamped with ill-conceived arbour-like devices that contribute little to their eventual situation.

THE ARBOUR IN BRITAIN

The arbour reached Britain, along with the legions, by 100 BC, and in our more temperate climate was probably used as much to escape from rain as a hot sun. However, illustrations showing solid roofs are rare and it would seem that the Romans learnt a lesson that is just as applicable today. This is simply that an open-sided arbour, with a solid top, sounds like thunder in anything but the lightest shower. You may remember a concerted advertising campaign to sell corrugated clear plastic roofing a few years ago. Unfortunately, apart from the noise problem, the top also tended to gather a thick layer of leaves and algae, neither of which improved the aesthetic qualities of the feature.

By the mid-sixteenth century the arbour had become an established garden feature. Still constructed from a framework of willow or juniper stems, it was planted with such unlikely material as rosemary, box or even cedar. The original framework soon decayed, leaving the living plants to form the structure, a technique that can be easily copied today.

Arbours continued to flourish in England right up to the great natural landscape school of the mid-eighteenth century. Then, along with virtually all the gardens that had gone before, they were swept away in the name of 'improvement' by Brown, Kent and Repton. Such men may well have created many parks of genius but they are considered by some, and I figure among them, to have practised a degree of vandalism. Certainly the sublime landscape was the order of the day, and it looks even finer with 200 years of careful husbandry, but the genuine glory of these pre-landscape gardens is gone forever and we are the poorer for it.

Of course it should be remembered that virtually all decorative gardens, as opposed to plots given over to food production, were the sole domain of rich landowners. The explosion of wealth that came with the Victorians changed all that, giving the new middle classes a new-found hobby. At last gardening became popular and so began an awareness of horticulture and the creation of an industry that is still expanding today.

VICTORIAN VALUES

The Victorians' problems and, coincidentally, delights came from a number of directions. First, with the development of towns and suburbs, it became obvious that the size of gardens had to be smaller, although one could still expect the average early villa to have anything from half to one and a half acres – practically an estate by today's standards! Towards the end of the nineteenth century this certainly became more restricted, but it meant that the pressures placed upon such spaces were enormous, bearing in mind both the new range of products from an Industrial Revolution and the wealth of plant material brought into the country by a new breed of botanists and collectors from around the world.

As far as style was concerned, there really

In this small town garden overhead beams give privacy from neighbouring windows.

Opposite: *A sitting area fits sensibly into the overall garden framework. Here is a delightful hooped arbour.*

was none and a dreadful compromise arose between the memories of the pre-landscape formal garden and the later informality of the great parks. Garden design books of the time suggested copying layouts based on carpets and tapestries. Currant-bun rockeries simulated an alpine scene, stagnant pools doubled for lakes and flower beds were cut out of turf in a range of crescents, diamonds and oblongs. The latter were filled with a prodigious range of half-hardy plants, reared in the new technology of conservatories and greenhouses. Such colour held sway for four or five months during the summer in a riot of good-humoured, if somewhat restless, taste.

But with all this intense activity came a glorious revival in every conceivable garden feature, whether it were buildings or monuments, statues or furniture, and with it too came the reintroduction of arbours and overheads of every description. As a rule the Victorians were convoluted and confused in the siting of these, and garden architecture had yet to find its way into a simpler, less cluttered and practical style. Iron hoops and structures of all kinds were popular, clothed with a preponderance of broad-leaved plants and ivy in particular. Pleaching, or the training of trees into a continuous line was an interesting feature, and could be used far more in gardens today.

ARBOURS TODAY

Some years ago I planned a modest country garden of something less than a half-acre and planted a ring of hornbeams (one of the best tree species for pleaching). Within this outer circle was set a carefully designed stone path, while in the middle a band of cobbles acted as host for a curved seat that looked out across another wing of the garden. Inside five years the carefully selected and pruned side branches had grown together, and in ten the tops of the hornbeams had been trained to lean in towards the middle to produce a fine dome through which sunlight could filter. The result was a living sculpture and a feature that could certainly be termed an arbour.

Another fascinating technique, although requiring patience, is the training of box or yew into a shelter. Yew, in particular, has attracted an undeservedly bad reputation for slow growth, but with the preparation of a well-manured trench and subsequent feeding, it can put on quite a respectable turn of speed. It is a fact that most people are happy to feed vegetables and the contents of a border but the poor old trees and hedges tend to get forgotten. They are, after all, plants like any other and gross feeders at that. Organic matter, forked in around the roots not only keeps them happy but prevents an adjacent bed from being drained of nourishment.

There is a delightful house in Cornwall that relies heavily on yew hedges for the division of space, and a degree of topiary. Several fine yews have been clipped into cones about 7.5 m (25 ft) high and subsequently hollowed out to form a shelter. Completely hidden within this, is a white seat that stands out in sharp relief to the virtually black interior. This is subtle yet surprising garden imagery at its best, and an idea that could be easily adapted to a smaller garden situation, given just a little patience. A word of warning though: yew, being slow to grow, is correspondingly amenable to clipping, needing a trim but once a year. At all costs resist using privet for such a feature which, although quick to establish, is not only a permanent millstone of maintenance but a glutton for nutrition at the expense of anything close by.

With the expansion of an Empire it was obvious that plant collectors would visit every part of the globe. This they did, bringing back new ideas as well as botanical specimens, from places like India, China and Japan. 'Chinoiserie', in particular, became very popular and we have a rich legacy of pavillions, pagodas and arbours in this oriental style. The latter were almost invariably built of cast iron and timber, and many would have looked equally at home as bandstands, part of a railway station or smothered in climbers in the corner of a garden. Foundaries sent out catalogues of literally hundreds of designs, although most tended to stay on the pages rather than behind the villa. In essence the distinguishing mark of an arbour is that it is open to the sky, or if not, that protection from the elements is minimal. In consequence the Victorian variety came with or without a solid roof, and the day of optional extras had arrived to stay.

Humour is an intrinsic part of garden design and there is far too much snobbery of a kind that is prejudiced against gnomes, certain sorts of plants that come in and out of fashion and garden architecture of unusual kinds. If somebody wants a gnome they should have one, and to blazes with those people that turn up their noses at alyssum and lobelia! It is all a matter of how and where you use them. What is considered bad taste can often be turned most successfully into a

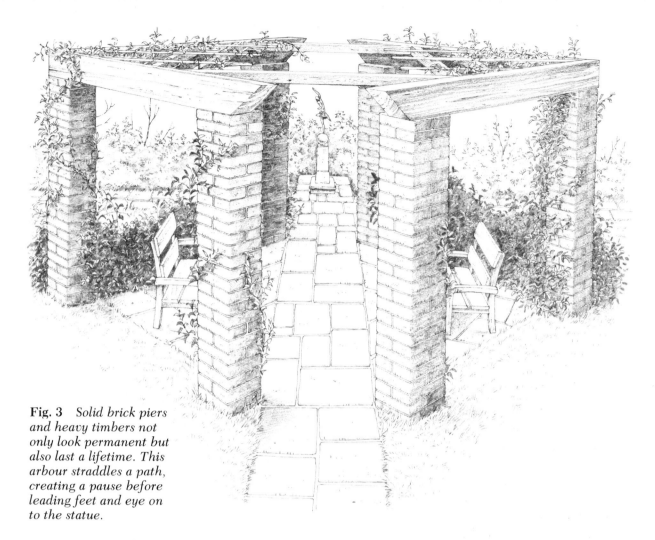

Fig. 3 *Solid brick piers and heavy timbers not only look permanent but also last a lifetime. This arbour straddles a path, creating a pause before leading feet and eye on to the statue.*

composition, and it looks all the better for it! For all their austerity, the Victorians were gloriously humorous and nowhere more so than in the garden. They had a habit of borrowing one style or feature and using it in another context altogether. One of my favourites is a totally charming but 'throw away' detail. It takes the form of a little tiled half-roof, about 2.4 m (8 ft) long, that is supported from an old stone wall in a distant corner of a garden. It still survives, which indicates the care and, no doubt, inherent cost of such a feature if built today. It gives little shelter but is enormous fun!

JEKYLL AND LUTYENS

This, perhaps, is the problem with virtually all garden architecture dating from this period. Fine it may be, but in the majority of cases cheap it is not. There are exceptions and

one can see fine examples in the wonderful books written by Gertrude Jekyll, both by herself and in conjunction with Lawrence Weaver. Jekyll is becoming something of a cult among upwardly mobile gardeners but this dubious privilege can in no way detract from the genius she wove into the grand and delicate frameworks created by Sir Edwin Lutyens. It would be quite impossible to show anything but a very few examples here, and in fairness most are quite out of scale for the confines of today's outside rooms.

The first of these, although of average size when measured against its contemporaries, would be large in anything but a generous garden today. It is clever because it is adaptable, and I built this same arrangement in a large town garden a number of years ago. The ground plan (Fig. 3) is such that there are six brick columns positioned around a square terrace constructed from old rectangular York stone. In two diagonally opposed arches there are single piers, but the corners boast two piers each and these are spaced far enough apart to allow a path to pass between them, continue through the arbour and pass out through the other two piers on the other side. This path gives a clear view of a well chosen statue that nestles in the planting at the end of the walk but before reaching it another path crosses at a right angle, unexpectedly leading both feet and eye off on another axis. It is an excellent example of surprise and ingenuity, two essential elements in garden design. Within the arbour two seats face each other. These are of generous proportions and constructed from stained hardwood to match the timber used in the open latticework above. The latter is built up in three stages, the first using heavy, shaped planks that link the supporting piers. The second stage takes lighter beams and these are set at a diagonal to the main framework, echoing the line of the path and paving below. Finally lathes are placed on top, running in the opposite direction, at right angles to the path. This produces a squared lattice effect that makes a delightful frame for the sky and an ideal host for climbers, in this case that superb thornless climbing rose Zephirine Drouhin, intertwined with the fragrance of summer flowering *Jasmine officinale*. Such an arbour is not difficult to build, although it requires a degree of skill and little more than a weekend with a bag of ready-mix cement!

The other great merit of Jekyll and many of her fellow gardeners is their attention to detail, something that is sadly lacking nearly a hundred years later. To detail was added strength, both of line and purpose. No diagrams are needed to imagine an arbour of modest size but massively constructed and, indeed, immensely strong. The original design had stone bases to the piers which would have been built off suitable concrete foundations. Today they could of course still be stone but an easier alternative would be blockwork, subsequently neatly rendered, or brickwork. The piers themselves are slightly narrower than the bases and built from roofing tiles, with a wide bed of mortar between

each course. The mortar is white rather than the normal dull grey and this does much to emphasize the darker tile and give the pattern greater intimacy. Cement additives are readily available but do steer clear of the awful tints of red, pink and green. They look ghastly in most situations. The heads of the piers are again capped with stone, which has been hand finished. Today, brickwork carefully laid would look almost as handsome. The timbers that form the main frame for the roof are gently cambered and would be ideally fashioned from elm, which is almost completely water resistant. Trellis forms the topmost layer, and panels can be easily bent to the slight radius, being nailed or screwed home. An alternative would be to drill the beams to accept galvanized wire, allowing ample scope for the tendrils of climbing plants such as clematis or passion flower.

ATTENTION TO DETAIL

It should be apparent by now that care taken in the design and building of an arbour is well rewarded. However, the pier, beams and overheads are only part of the picture, and these act only as an open roof to the floor below. Traditionally, immense care was taken with this area and the tired jumble of crazy-paving or cracked slabs so often seen today just will not do. The floor of this last Victorian example would echo the delicacy of the tile piers and might consist of herringbone brickwork, the colour of which is closely matched to the tiles. The bricks should be laid on edge and, as this is an essentially 'busy' design, the whole broad panel is possibly surrounded by a band of solid rectangular stonework, which in turn links with the stone bases of the piers themselves. Nothing is left to chance. It is a well thought out scheme that relies for effect on simplicity and that is the essence of good design.

While this period of garden design had a great deal to commend it, it also had its dark

This little arch is closed off to accept the charming white wrought iron seat. Planting is undemonstrative but subtle.

side, and in the area of arbours and overheads the use of so called 'rustic' work became popular. This utilized soft wood, usually larch with the bark left on, and was cheap, quick and easy to erect. In all but the rarest situation it did, and still does, look tatty. Places where it can work include the ultimately informal parts of a garden or where it is completely dominated by planting.

The idea is originally a mediterranean one and harks back to the cultivation of vines. Here an arbour is simply a framework of relatively thin poles which more often than not are replaced every year. A rather more permanent arrangement uses rubble piers that are subsequently plastered with poles resting, lattice fashion on top. A largely frost free climate extends the life of the piers and any such treatment in this country would necessitate rendering in place of plaster. There is no doubt, however, that the shadows cast by overhead timbers of any kind produce fascinating patterns, particularly in an area where sunlight is both bright and strong. In our more temperate land the effect is slighter, but nevertheless one that can be used to good advantage and produce subtle results in a given location.

Having said that rustic work is not suitable for small contemporary gardens there is always an exception.

TOWN GARDEN

Fig. 4 shows a town garden dominated by high brick walls. The boundaries are both rectangular and oppressive, and the brief was for a design that could, if possible, provide at least a hint of rural fresh air and detract from the almost inevitable feeling of claustrophobia.

The first job was to consider the basic ground plan and here I decided to turn the whole pattern at 45° to the house. Paving was a combination of neat Cotswold colour, random rectangular slabs teamed with brick, the

latter matching those used in the house as closely as possible. The main terrace or 'patio' area led out from the sliding doors, while the smallest space under the kitchen window was given over to a raised bed, predominantly for annual 'instant' colour. This interlocked with a herb bed that was framed with low-growing *Santolina incana*. Grass was considered impractical in such a small area, so paving extends across the full width of the garden. Between this and the arbour lies an area of loose cobbles, gravel and a number of carefully selected boulders. These provide not only an attractive change of texture, particularly in conjunction with bold foliaged plants, but at the same time disguise a quite awful array of manholes. The latter are a builder's delight, nearly always in an awkward place and turned at an infuriating angle to the house to make paving around them particularly difficult. Covers can sometimes be turned to match the paving, or you can buy recessed covers that resemble a tray into which a suitably matching concrete can be poured to match the terrace as a whole. Never try and disguise a manhole with a pot, sundial, birdbath or statue; this simply draws the eye and emphasizes the cover. If it's in a lawn, just leave it alone and hopefully no-one will notice it. In this garden the boulders sit comfortably on the covers, reinforced with low ground cover and cobbles. In the event of an emergency, roll the boulders back, part the ground cover and get on with the job.

In this composition garden walls serve as both hosts to a wide range of climbing plants and a direct design link with the rooms inside the house. To achieve this, the one running out from the kitchen has been colour-washed to a similar tone as that inside, increasing the feeling of space and leading the eye out towards the arbour. The latter really is the key to the whole garden and in such a limited space it has a great deal of work to do in both visual and practical terms. In order to enhance the rural connotations it was decided not to use crisp squared timbers that would be the natural choice. Instead I chose rustic

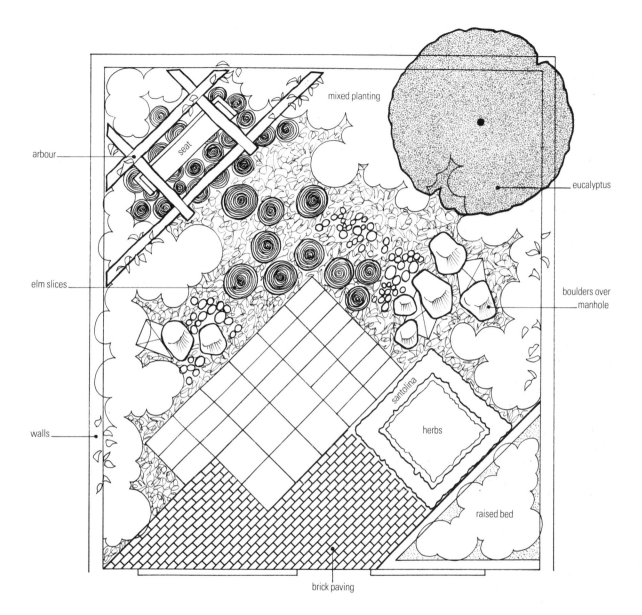

Fig. 4 *Another approach for a small garden is to turn the whole design at 45 degrees: crisp bricks and precast slabs give way to a softer treatment of log stepping stones, ground cover and a rustic arbour.*

timbers but with the bark removed to minimize decay and discourage the build up of fungal spores and the eventual transmission of disease. The posts were sanded down and given two coats of a non toxic wood preservative. Remember *never* to use creosote, which is poisonous to plants and animals alike.

The area beneath the arbour is to play host to an old iron seat, painted white with wooden slats, in the best park bench tradition. This will be placed on a number of timber slices, sawn out of large diameter elm trunks. These are splendidly informal and can be used for stepping-stones as well as butted together to form a very 'rural' paving pattern. The remaining space under and around the beams will be given over to shade-tolerant woodland shrubs and hardy perennials that

will thrive in the angle formed by the north-facing walls.

The first job is to provide support for the uprights and a practical solution is to sink lengths of glazed drain pipe, approximately 600 mm × 100 mm (2 ft × 4 in), into the ground. Check these are vertical by inserting a post and using a spirit level. When they are true, carefully backfill around the drain with crushed stone or well-broken, clean hardcore. This will prevent movement once the structure is in place. The poles themselves will be fractionally less than 100 mm (4 in) and if they are oversize carefully shave them down to achieve a snug fit. The overall height will be approximately 2.8 m (8 ft 6 in), this allowing 600 mm (2 ft) in the ground. Cut the ends of the poles where they will meet and use galvanized nails of ample length. To-

Opposite: Timber is the most versatile constructional material. Here a simple arch is smothered with roses, although maintenance of the framework will be a problem.

This arbour is all the more effective for being at the top of a slight change of level. The all-embracing roses do much to soften the outline of the construction.

gether with cross-bracing and firm ground this anchoring will produce an arbour that should last for many years. The log slices that play host to the seat are approximately 75 mm (3 in) thick and can be bedded on a simple foundation of well compacted gravel or ballast.

PLANTING THE ARBOUR

Planting will need to be atmospheric and this might include *Garrya elliptica* 'Skimmia' and *Philadelphus* 'Belle Etoile' as shrubs to provide form and structure. Hardy perennials might include *Polygonatum multiflorum* (Solomon's seal), *Convallaria majalis* (lily of the valley), and the male fern *Dryopteris filix-mas*. As far as climbers for the arbour and the adjacent walls are concerned, these too will need to be shade tolerant. My own favourite self-clinging climber in this situation is *Parthenocissus henryana*, a Virginia creeper that is slightly less rampant than the type. It has a most attractive foliage, with veins picked out in ivory – all the more telling in a shady spot. It has the virtue of brilliant red foliage in the

autumn, and to my mind its tracery of stems in winter have architectural beauty. Clematis, contrary to popular belief, do exceptionally well in shade and that old favourite 'Nellie Moser', with its early flowering pink blooms, is one of the best. However, for a longer display choose the remarkable *Clematis tangutica* with its delicate yellow bells that appear in midsummer. The bonus of this clematis, like the wild 'Old Man's Beard', is in the seeds with their feathery, silky heads. This means there is a worthwhile display for between three and four months, which is excellent value.

On the side of the arbour closest to the house there is more light available, and in a confined garden one can afford to plant for fragrance. Some people find honeysuckle just a little overpowering but for my money it is delicious. The best for spectacular flower is probably *Lonicera × americana* with its enormous trusses of white to deeply yellow blossom and pervading perfume. Another real favourite of mine is *Jasmine officinale* with white flowers and delicious scent. Easy to grow and hardy, it should belong to every garden.

When you consider the size of this arbour, nestling in the corner formed by the walls, and when you appreciate the short time needed to establish both shrubs and climbers, it soon becomes obvious that the method of support is almost incidental. The arbour is a vehicle for the plant material arranged over and around it. As soon as you grasp this fact you will understand the importance of simplicity. Fussy poles, convoluted iron work and nonsensical roofs detract from the delicacy of flower and foliage. Such frippery may be much beloved by horticultural buyers of garden centre chains but it does little justice to the garden in which it appears. The arbour we have just looked at really forms the corner piece of an entire garden; it is part of and sets the theme for all around it. A larger garden or smaller overhead structure changes the emphasis and produces an incidental feature rather than a dominant focal point.

FORMING A FOCUS

A small arbour can emphasize the junction of two paths running at right angles to one another. This type of design is simple but effective, with the topmost beams pitched to form a roof-like canopy. This has the advantage of creating a feeling of space and importance to the point in question. Such beams can be stained black, another precise statement which brings drama to the planting of a pale blossom such as the lovely climbing rose 'Swan Lake'. A gravel path below is just right, edged with bricks, with the adjacent lawn being kept at a slightly higher level to facilitate mowing.

This arrangement is a traditional device, but one that is as fresh today as ever it was. Perhaps one of the most telling examples is in the glorious white garden at Sissinghurst Castle in Kent. Here Vita Sackville-West produced what has been described 'the most beautiful garden at Sissinghurst, and indeed of all England'. Surrounded by fine old mellow brick walls all the planting is of white, grey and silver, including *Lilium regale*, white delphiniums, artemesia, stachys and the striking 'Silver Willow' leaved pear *Pyrus salicifolia* 'Pendula'. Brick paths flanked by low box hedges contain the planting, giving form to the herbaceous species that could look untidy without definition. The four paths converge to the middle of the garden where a charming arbour is smothered in white roses. Without this central feature that acts as a pivot, the garden might well appear flat and the arbour balances the vertical strength provided by the surrounding walls.

OVERHEAD BEAMS

Up until now we have really been considering the arbour in its traditional role, one that forms a vehicle for plants and a secluded shelter for sitting. In the modern garden the emphasis is changing and overhead beams of crisp, sawn and planed timber serve a slightly different purpose. Here they are becoming a visual extension of the house itself, echoing an architectural line and providing definition for the sitting area below. More often than not they extend from the building itself, or are close to it, but more occasionally they might be used in a more distant part of a garden to tie a particular feature into the overall composition.

If we remain on the theme of small urban gardens we can see how the modern overhead can be used to excellent advantage (Fig. 5). The overall measurements of this particular plot are 7.5 m × 6 m (25 ft × 20 ft), tiny even by today's compressed housing standards. Ugly concrete block walls form the main boundaries and all in all the proposition is uncompromising. The owners were young but keen gardeners and this was their first home. They required maturity in their planting as soon as possible, ample room to sit and entertain, and also a working area separated from the main garden, where they could store tools and carry on the basic jobs of propagation, potting and general plant care. Such an area can be a real asset in cramped urban properties where storage space within the house is at a premium.

The first job was the basic allocation of space, and this was complicated by the rear of the house facing north. To overcome this problem the main sitting area was planned at the far end of the garden, and in order to give this definition it was decided to run a new concrete block wall at right angles to the bottom boundary, back towards the house. This would separate the utility area from the decorative part of the garden and increase

Fig. 5 *Contemporary gardens need crisp detailing and a no nonsense style. Brick paving and solid railway sleepers are echoed at a higher level by simple stained timbers that carry over to form the roof of a potting bench.*

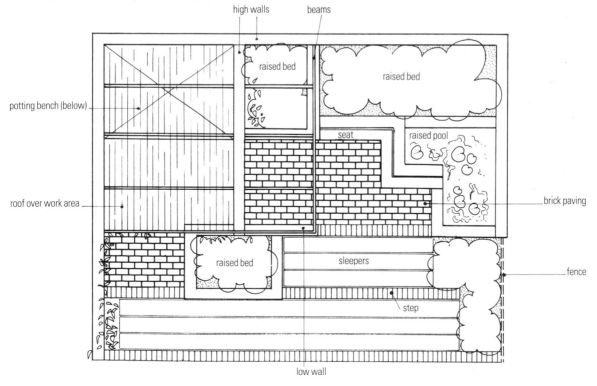

the element of shelter. The walls themselves were painted a soft cream (Remember that white paint produces a harsh glare in all but the softest light). Lower walls and raised beds, built from mellow old stock bricks further subdivide the space, while to one side a raised pool fitted with an unobtrusive bubble jet fountain creates a tranquil feature.

The paving is a combination of railway sleepers and brick, the latter also using old stocks but only those that have been well fired and therefore able to resist frost. The brick therefore is a unifying element, used as coping on all the walls and producing a softer line on top of the painted block walls in particular. A built-in seat links the low brick dividing wall and the higher wall in the centre of the garden and this also provides anchorage for the black painted section of scaffold pole that supports one end of the overhead canopy. The canopy itself is very straightforward utilizing solid 23 cm × 5 cm (9 in × 2 in) floor joists, stained to an attractive pale brown. For support they are keyed back into the brick coping which will help prevent the timber twisting. The scaffold pole is plugged at the top with a wooden dowel, a double-ended screw joining this and the beams together. This beam nearest the house is in fact carried across the end of the wall, becoming the front of the potting bench. The latter is cleverly designed and after all, why should such areas be boring? The horizontal timbers echo the line of the overhead beams as does the bench itself. The raised bed and generous planting gives space division between the two sides of the garden and brings a decorative air to the more austere utility area. Such walls and timbers cry out for planting and climbers in particular. Foliages with an architectural line is ideal, and rheum, acers, dracaenas, hostas and Phormium will thrive and give boldness to a sheltered space. For the beams

Modern garden architecture is far from clinical; here bold foliage plants soften the positive line of brick paving and railway sleepers. The stained brown beams contrast with the cream walls.

wisteria is an ideal choice, as it is both vigorous and easily trained. It is in fact such a strong twiner that flimsy overheads can be quickly distorted and even broken – our stout 23 cm × 5 cm (9 in × 2 in) timbers are ideal. Both *Wisteria floribunda* (Japanese wisteria) and *Wisteria sinensis* (Chinese wisteria) will produce spectacular racemes of pale blue flowers early in the year, at the end of May and throughout June, with a second less spectacular flush later in the season if you are lucky. Once established they can quickly become rampant and, if necessary, should be pruned hard in winter to keep them under control. Bear in mind, however, that drastic cutting will also endanger flowering, so do not remove all the wood that will produce the new flowering shoots. Wisteria blossom can also be subject to attack by birds, just as the buds are forming and ready to open.

TRADITIONAL

As a direct contrast in style, look at the arbour in the photograph on p. 34. This too is a modern arrangement but uses wonderful old cast iron columns rescued from a demolition site. The pretty lattice roof soars upwards to a pinnacle and plays host to a healthy passion flower, the perfect foil, with its waxen flowers, to the delicacy of the iron work. A sitting area of Old York stone nestles below while planting wraps itself around the whole set piece. One of the advantages of an arbour is the very fact that it is open to the sky and planting from adjoining borders can encroach or even continue right below the canopy. The wire racks incorporated underneath are also an attractive and unusual idea. These are built set back in tiers, one above the other, giving room for a fine display of pots that would provide seasonal colour throughout the year.

White paint is both a traditional and practical feature here, as it really allows the tracery of metal to stand out against the darker green foliage behind. A rampant climber like passiflora can be taken down during repainting, and it will benefit from a haircut at the same time to thin out the inevitable tangled branches.

Choosing the right furniture for this sort of arbour is also desperately important and the folly of garish plastic, or even rustic timbers should be obvious. The ideal is good wrought iron (not the imitation plastic kind which looks what it is). White is better than black and if you are really into good design then use a plain tablecloth and pretty scatter cushions, but remember to remove them at night and in the event of rain!

This arbour is placed at the bottom of the garden but the really charming possibility is to extend the main supporting beams under the canopy right the way across the plot to link into an identical structure on the other side. Not only would this be a marvellous way of opening up a relatively narrow space, it would also allow each sitting area, if the aspect were suitable, to be bathed in sun at different times of the day.

An arbour with a similar flavour, although constructed in timber, is shown in Fig. 6. This would not be easy to build and is really the province of the craftsman joiner. We talked of humour earlier in this section and this quite lovely structure is romantic rather than practical. It does indeed charm the eye and if the woodwork is stained, the tented interior, swagged up at the corners to allow entry, would stand out in sharp relief.

These free standing arbours are not so much quiet retreats as focal points, around which a garden can radiate in much the same way as the spokes of a wheel. Their function is altogether different, more showy and, apart from strict design criteria, less useful.

Another similar arbour is shown on p. 35, this time built almost entirely from trellis. The art of 'treillage' has all but died out in today's domestic garden, largely because of the intricacy and cost of the work involved. A hundred years ago it held full sway with entire garden areas being built from trellis

Fig. 6 *Fantasy is an integral part of garden design and this tented arbour could be straight out of a medieval joust. It would fit equally well as a slightly pretentious focal point in any upwardly mobile composition.*

patterns woven in delicate and intricate shapes. Such an arbour is most definitely rural, acting as an important focal point in any country garden. White paint is the obvious choice here and planting should always be selected carefully. Remember to use plants in drifts, rather than as individual specimens. I think I'd go further than the scheme shown here and use lavender as a low frame to pink bush roses at an intermediate level. Climbing roses and clematis should twist their way through the white lattice work, leading the eye gently towards the roof and a delicate finial that acts as a top knot at the highest point. A final and most important statement could be provided by a statue placed within, reminding us that an arbour must always have a purpose, whether for sitting, or as the setting for a beautiful ornament.

MIXING MATERIALS

Mixing constructional materials is not always easy, or necessarily called for, as ease of building and simplicity of design can often be threatened as a consequence. However, it can work, as shown in the pretty arbour on p. 38. This particular design takes up the corner of a formal garden laid out along the lines of those great pre-landscape gardens of the seventeenth century. It is not difficult to construct, with the lower timber sections being built from simple upright beams and arched top pieces. Sections of the trellis, which could be bought from any garden centre, fill in all the gaps apart from the entrance, while the wrought iron roof, although the province of a blacksmith, is not overly complicated. Once again such a feature is of considerable size and would need careful positioning in a garden of modest proportions. But there is ample room for sitting and the reconstituted stone seats are in keeping with the tradition design. The floor too is laid with painstaking care, using a combination of brick edging and small cobbles. The latter should be laid as closely together as possible, like eggs in a crate. The dreadful municipal tendency to use them 'currant bun' fashion degrades the material and makes walking over them uncomfortable in the extreme.

As a final point, see how the timber has weathered down to a mature silvery grey. This usually means that a coat of preservative is in order, but it is one of the best colours in the garden for associating with virtually any plant material.

CONTEMPORARY ALTERNATIVES

Romance is something that is inseparable from all good gardens, traditional or contemporary, and it is largely the grouping and

Opposite: *This tented arbour is constructed from a tracery of metalwork, the passion flower sprawling over the delicate roof.*

The path and low hedges emphasize the linear nature of this arbour's design, drawing both feet and eye through the space.

selection of plants that bring the romantic composition to life. Fig. 7 shows one of my recent gardens which, while planted to take full advantage of our temperate climate, relies heavily on the uncluttered style prevalent in Scandinavia and on the West Coast of America.

It is a garden of modest proportions, measuring 13.5 m × 16.5 m (45 ft × 55 ft) and is designed specifically as an outside room in the fullest sense. The site had certain complications, not least a north facing aspect and a gentle but steady slope up from the house. The brief was simple: room for sitting, dining and entertaining, a summer house, a strong element of water, and planting to draw the whole composition together. In addition the latter had to be as maintenance free as possible.

As the slope was even the first element was to introduce a series of level terraces. To create a feeling of width the paving of both brick and precast concrete slabs was laid in a stretcher bond across the garden and this was emphasized by butting the slabs end to end, but raking out the joints between each row.

Each terrace is separated by long, broad pools and to highlight their importance the only access up the garden is by stepping stones across the water. The steps are generous and each feature is staggered, again to increase the apparent width.

The main sitting area opens out from the brick-built summerhouse and in the corner of the garden, to provide shelter and screening from a bad view, I built a high brick wall. This ensures an ideal support for the unashamedly modern arbour. This structure is pure architecture and echoes the clean lines of the largely timber house on the other side of the terrace. Because it is large, the timbers need to be correspondingly proportioned and I have used sturdy 10 cm × 10 cm (4 in × 4 in) planed posts as supports for the main frame. These are sandwiched first by 23 cm × 5 cm (9 in × 2 in) planed floor joists that run back to the brick wall and lastly by 30 cm × 5 cm (12 in × 2 in) beams that run across the front and middle of the feature, providing a beautifully proportioned line that sits at right angles to the main axis of the garden.

The final set of timbers is much lighter,

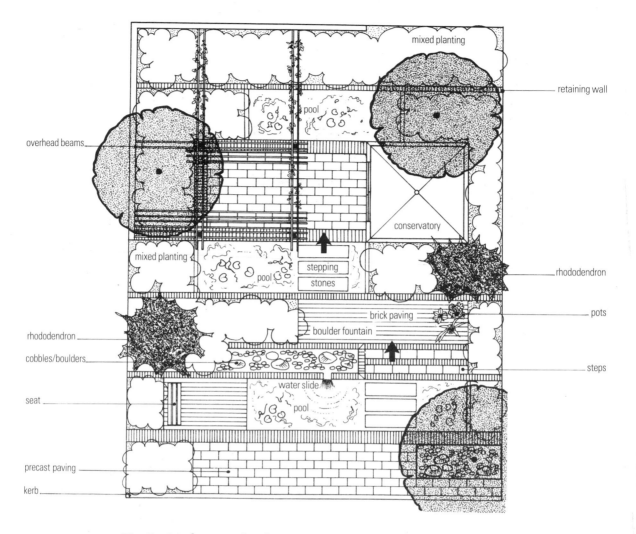

Fig. 7 *Modern garden design should never compromise. Here a superbly detailed arbour helps to balance the volume of the pool and the height of the summerhouse, planting softening the overall concept.*

measuring 5 cm × 5 cm (2 in × 2 in) and are screwed to the underside of the 30 cm × 5 cm (12 in × 2 in) beams. It is this final set that gives the whole design both intimacy and enclosure. The number of slats can be reduced or increased to provide a lesser or greater degree of shade, but the shadow patterns set up by them are superb and become an integral part of the design sequence, moving across the terrace throughout the day.

Against such a dominant line planting is vital, acting as a complementary element rather than a softening influence. Broad-leaved shrubs and the striking forms of

coniferous plants are the idea. For climbers try the great ornamental vine *Vitis coignetiae* (Japanese crimson glory vine), or the hardy fruiting variety *Vitis riparia* (riverbank grape). The latter has the bonus of charmingly fragrant flowers that smell of mignonette, and what could be more pleasant than picking the freely produced black grapes? Brandt is another edible variety that colours superbly in the autumn. A final choice might be the Teinturer grape, *Vitis vinifera* 'Purpurea'. At the beginning of the summer, the leaves are a reddish brown, turning to a rich purple in autumn.

It is always a temptation to use any over-

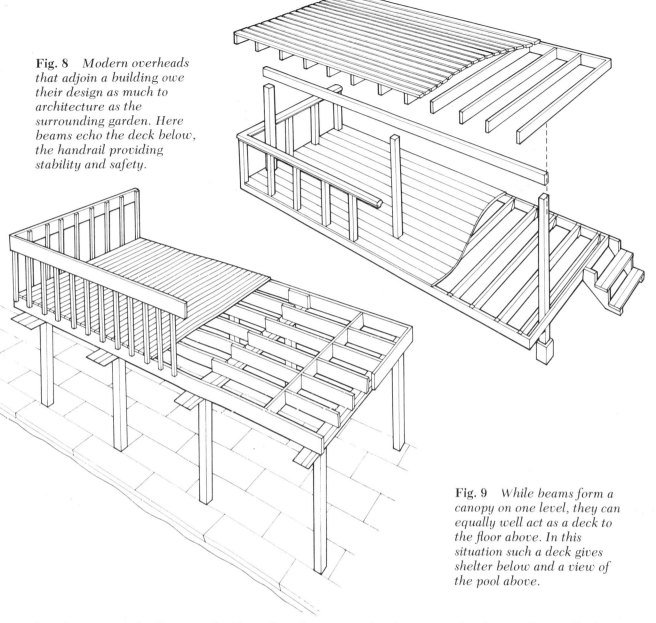

Fig. 8 *Modern overheads that adjoin a building owe their design as much to architecture as the surrounding garden. Here beams echo the deck below, the handrail providing stability and safety.*

Fig. 9 *While beams form a canopy on one level, they can equally well act as a deck to the floor above. In this situation such a deck gives shelter below and a view of the pool above.*

head structure for hanging baskets, but the golden rule is *don't*. All they do is clutter an inherently simple device and inevitably are placed at such a height as to catch the unwary a severe blow to the temple. If you want planting, let a climber do the job. There is sometimes a problem getting them to cling to the upright supports, but the best solution is to use neat plastic-coated wire. Either run two or three strands from top to bottom, tucking the plant in as it grows, or tack galvanized eyes at regular intervals up the posts, looping similar wire around the timbers as necessary. A similar technique can if necessary be used on top of the arbour.

The lesson to be learnt from all these arbours is that they are specifically designed for the areas they are to serve, built in context and part of the garden framework. They are not, unlike so many of the 'off the peg' varieties, just dumped in isolation in the hope they will look pretty. Timber overheads can link naturally with a timber deck and if the latter is suspended to give ample air circulation, then the problem of decay can be virtually non existent. This combination often looks at its best on a steeply sloping hillside site where the deck can be cantilevered out over the drop on timber, brick or concrete piers. South-facing hillside sites can also be

very sunny, and it is often necessary to shade both a sitting area and the rooms adjoining the deck, to reduce heat gain and prevent fabrics from fading. A simple but effective design is shown in Fig. 8 and should not be beyond the capabilities of any reasonable carpenter. Well seasoned and treated softwood would be quite acceptable in the situation, and the sturdy handrail matches the visual strength of the main uprights as well as containing the decked area. Steps have been kept relatively narrow to eliminate possible accidents, but in a situation where the drop at the end of the terrace was minimal they could be designed to run the full width, always a generous statement.

If we carry the deck and arbour to its logical conclusion then we arrive at the arrangement shown in Fig. 9 which adjoins a swimming pool. In this case the deck, leading away from upstairs French windows, becomes the roof of the arbour below. This must be the ultimate link between house and landscape and a perfect excuse for encouraging rampant climbers to merge the two levels so that it becomes almost impossible to separate them. The views from the upper deck could be stunning, and one of the important lessons to be learnt here is the utilization of really heavy timbers. All too often modern overheads are built from undersized beams which look far too flimsy and, incidentally, appear taller than they really are.

AWAY FROM THE HOUSE

Although most modern arbours look their best adjoining, or at least close to, a house, a well detailed structure can look excellent some way away where it can provide emphasis and shade to a specific area. The reason they often look awkward is because of

Not every garden can accommodate an arbour of this size but where space allows such a focal point is genuinely impressive.

39

their austerity, good with architecture but not so good without. I am one of those people hooked on outdoor barbecuing and nothing to my mind can beat that tantalizing aroma of steak, sausage and onion. I am also convinced, against all the recommendations of the manufacturers, that good old-fashioned charcoal or, even better, apple or pear logs beat hands down the ultra modern, gas-fired, ceramic coal types. However, my kind of barbecuing is sometimes temperamental and nearly always smoky, certainly in the initial stages, and bearing this in mind I heartily support an opinion that relegates the barbecue away from outside the French windows, even if it is a longer walk from the kitchen. However, one of the problems of eating outside and away from the shade of buildings is, surprisingly enough, too much sun. The glare on a white tablecloth can be almost intolerable and the advantages of an arbour or crisp 'overhead' is self evident.

Siting a barbecue, or any sitting area for that matter, creates a major influence on the garden pattern as a whole. Not only will it need paths for access, it will also need ample space for sitting and to carry out the cooking. These functions need to be kept separate to give the diners the added pleasure of watching the cook work.

In design terms it is always attractive to 'hang' a scheme on some established feature within the garden. Mature trees are ideal and, in the arrangement shown in Fig. 10, an old apple tree sits comfortably at one end of the composition. Barbecues are alfresco affairs and the built-in seat is large enough to take trays of food, cushions and at least half a dozen people. Off duty, it doubles as an excellent play area.

The raised bed and barbecue interlock with the seat, and the latter also gives support on one side to the slatted overhead. This can be cleverly built so that one end nudges its way up into the branches of the old fruit tree. This has the effect of linking the elements together, removing austerity from one and adding vitality to the other. It is a delicate

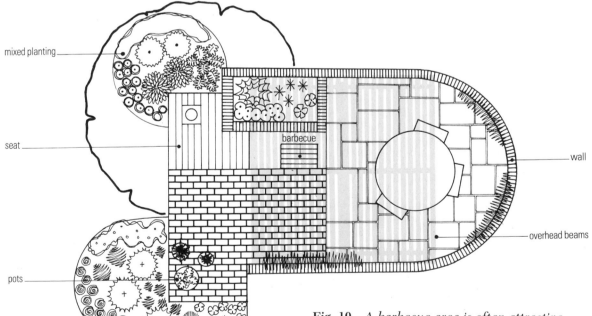

Fig. 10 *A barbecue area is often attractive sited away from the house, preferably in a position that catches evening sun. Overhead beams here help to define the sitting area and balance the height of the tree.*

mixed planting

seat

pots

wall

overhead beams

barbecue

framework of thin open slats (Fig. 11) and, as such, has an airy presence that allows a greater feeling of light and air to enter the space below. In order to contain the sitting area a low wall approximately 1 m (3 ft 6 in) high wraps itself around the old York stone paving in a strong flowing curve, the outer band of planting reinforcing the line and tempering what amounts to a large 'hard landscape' feature. The arbour is carried right over both the barbecue and sitting area, with the end supports softened by climbers that rise from the semi-circle of planting at the far end.

Another, perhaps less obvious, advantage of any arbour of this type is the fact that in the event of rain a sheet or tarpaulin can be quickly and easily thrown over the top and tied down securely to the timber uprights. Such action can save the day and retain a party atmosphere in even the worst thunderstorm!

A second even simpler set of beams are shown on p. 42. These are run out from a high brick wall that divides the utility side of the garden from the decorative. The beams are supported by joist hangers on one side and crisp square section steel to the other. The timbers are once again 23 cm × 5 cm (9 in × 2 in), this time planed and painted white. At the front end simple halving joints allow the cross members to protrude, and it really is important to keep these uncut. Resist the temptation so beloved by landscape gardening firms to 'nose' them off, leaving an unsympathetic angle. In some situations this can work, and we will see how in the section that deals with arches and pergolas, but here the architectural crispness of line is all important and the beams look the better for it.

IN THE SUBURBS

But after looking at all these individual examples and before leaving the subject of arbours altogether let us consider one last

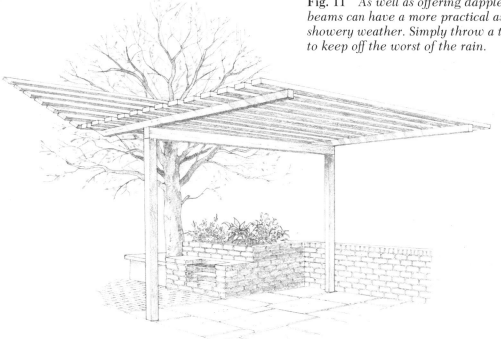

Fig. 11 *As well as offering dappled shade beams can have a more practical aspect in showery weather. Simply throw a tarpaulin over to keep off the worst of the rain.*

To produce a clean and simple line these beams are precisely constructed and jointed – providing a perfect host to climbing plants.

suburban garden. Let us see how it has been planned not only to take full advantage of the site but also how the arbour fits into the pattern to fulfil a double role. This garden is very narrow, backing on to a row of terraced houses that could be in any of a thousand locations scattered across the country. Although having the basic shape (Fig. 12) as the plot illustrated in our design section it is considerably smaller – a real headache in both design and cultural terms!

Like so many of its counterparts access is by a lower basement level, in this case the kitchen, and here the main problem is to maximize a meagre light source. White chippings are ideal for this, obtaining maximum reflection from the surrounding whitewashed walls. Stepping-stones lead through the gravel, and steps climb to the main terrace level where there is ample room for sitting, dining and sunbathing. Walls flank either side of the garden and these form the perfect starting point for raised beds which wrap this patio in flower and foliage. In a family garden one of these could quite easily be converted into a sandpit, and remember too that as far as toddlers are concerned raised pools are often much safer than those at ground level.

Here climbers soften contemporary overheads which reflect their immediate surroundings – underlying design is unashamedly modern.

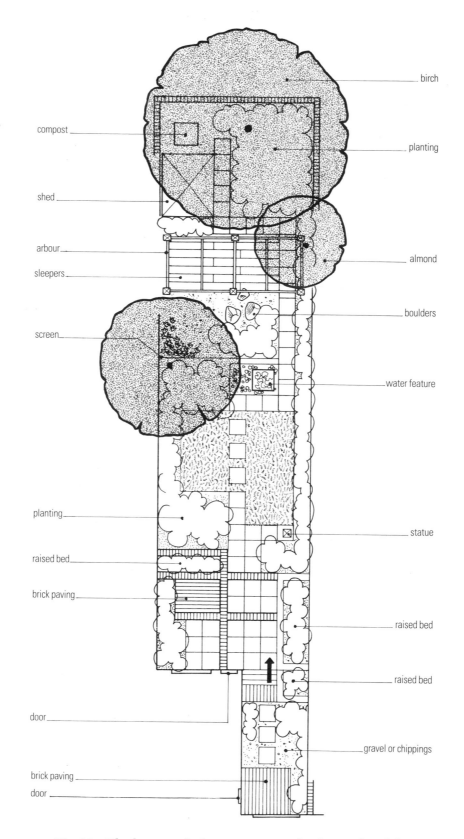

birch

planting

compost

almond

shed

arbour

sleepers

boulders

screen

water feature

planting

statue

raised bed

brick paving

raised bed

raised bed

door

gravel or chippings

brick paving

door

Fig. 12 *The beauty of a long narrow garden lies in the ability to create individual garden 'rooms'. Here the most distant area centres around a delightful arbour, with old oak beams and brick piers.*

The two raised beds at the front of the terrace act as a 'tension point', compressing the space and enclosing the paved area before we move into the next garden room. Here there is certainly room for a small rectangular lawn which, again, would be ideal for play and a good deal softer on young knees than slabs or gravel. Stepping-stones cross the grass and these have been set just below the turf to allow easy mowing. Once across the lawn the path turns through a right angle, taking us across to the extreme boundary and helping to create a feeling of maximum width. In the new angle formed by the slabs sits a water feature – a smooth square of slate. This has been set over an old water tank, a hole drilled through the middle and water recirculated by a submersible pump. The result is both fascinating and child-proof. To reinforce the division between the garden rooms a trellis spans virtually the whole width, extending the line of a fine old pear tree.

The final room is a total surprise from the neat lawn and terrace just left behind. Here is a cottage garden with no lawn, just soft old-fashioned plants of verbascum, hollyhocks, cotton lavender and rosemary growing through a golden gravel surface. The afternoon sun lingers here on a fine arbour in the traditional English style. It reaches from side to side of the garden, forming an arch to the right, and under which the path leads to the shed. The piers are of mellow old brick, the beams of weathered oak. This is neither crisp nor rustic; it is solidly built for the purpose of scrambling roses, clematis and fragrant jasmine. The rear of the left hand set of piers has been closed in, using old elm boards and this comfortably screens the shed and compost

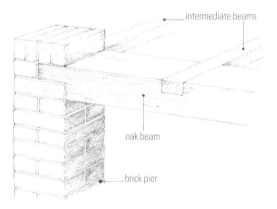

Fig. 13 *Where strength is vital, solid brick piers offer the perfect anchor, as well as visual stability.*

beyond. The constructional details are simple: the beams that run between the piers have been let into the brickwork, while the intermediate cross members are notched over the main beams (Fig. 13). The elm boards are simply nailed to battens, bolted to the rear of the piers. To continue the theme of solidity the paving beneath the arbour is laid in railway sleepers, these fine old baulks of timber, almost indefinitely resisting decay and rot. The joints have been left slightly open, soil brushed in, and low-spreading thymes allowed to colonize.

So, despite a pedigree of many thousands of years, the arbour remains a highly adaptable garden feature. Formal, informal, rustic or contemporary, it can suit like a glove the service to which it is put. But treat such adaptability with respect. There is nothing worse, or more lacking in taste, than a clash of styles brought about by simple insensitivity.

3

Pergolas and Arches

Arbours and overheads are by their very nature primarily static features. By that I mean they encourage one to sit and linger, or at least concentrate a particular activity in a specific area.

Pergolas and arches are quite different and one of their main functions is to provide transition from one place to another. In other words, unlike an arbour, they go somewhere. Whether that going is effective, whether it provides climax, surprise or a gentle excuse just to slow down is dependent upon the design, siting and overall concept of what is a wonderfully adaptable garden feature.

To most of us they have an undeniably English flavour and it is quite true that they have been an inseparate part of our garden architecture for a long time. Such has been their popularity since the Victorian revolution that they are undoubtedly the most prolific free-standing garden features. Few backyards and even fewer grand estates are without one, two or even more. The problem with familiarity however is an unfortunate degree of contempt and this is self evident on any train journey. Here one can see within the space of a few minutes a disastrous array of half-baked super structures dotted at random across a multitude of lawns, borders and vegetable plots.

It is a fact that no feature, for a feature it most certainly should be, suffers more from neglect and poor positioning. It needs dignity, it needs a place to go and above all it needs excellent, if only simple construction. The difference between an arch and pergola is simply one of degree. The arch is a scene setter, a transitional tension point which one encounters for a moment and then passes on. A pergola is a drawn out affair and I use the word in a romantic sense. One can easily fall in love with this feature, with the perfume of its climbers, with its persuasive meander and

perhaps most of all for its stability that provides a vital part of the garden framework in summer and winter alike.

EARLY DAYS

Although most of us consider it to be an indigenous product, it has a history dating back to the very first civilization and in the early days, its purpose and form was virtually synonymous with the arbour.

The creation of gardens really heralds the maturity of any civilization, as it assumes social stability and a well organized hierarchy. As we have seen, many gardens served a dual purpose, to include both decorative elements and the straightforward cultivation of certain crops. In practice these operations became blurred, and with the eventual passing of time visual pleasure outstripped food production and the latter was relegated to areas further from the house or secondary residential buildings.

From the very earliest times religions and mythical symbolism governed the construction of gardens. The further east one moves the more obvious this becomes. Egypt, Persia and Mesopotamia, while adhering to a degree of mysticism, were equally interested in the social opportunities such space provided. In the Far East, first China and then Japan used the garden almost entirely for meditation. While the latter were based on landscape patterns the former, middle eastern gardens were far more stylized and geometric in design. The most recurrent theme is the cruciform and this is copied over and over in both Persian carpets and their incomparable glorietta gardens. Water in the form of pools or longer canals form the cross with walks, paved areas and planting, filling the rectan-

Larch poles are not always the most suitable material for pergolas, being prone to rapid decay. This squared canopy forms a superb host for a canopy of mellow foliage.

47

gles between. Such patterns tend towards symmetry, and in the Egyptian garden it was easy to allocate individual parts of the rectangles to a different crop: dates, pomegranates, figs and of course the ubiquitous vine. The latter by its twining nature was nearly always grown on arbours and pergolas. The latter, being longer than an arbour, offering more space and an incidental greater degree of shade.

There is a fascinating example of Egyptian garden design dating from 1400 BC, showing quite clearly many features with which we are familiar today. Pools, arbours, trees and walling play important roles, while the main centre section is given over to grapes grown on long parallel pergolas.

This basically formal style pervaded throughout the Greek and Roman periods and was still prevalent in England where Tudor gardens were laid out to an inevitably regular pattern. Here pergolas took the form of long walks either from side to side, crossing in the middle or skirting the perimeter. They were often punctuated by arbours which rose above the general level and acted as meeting places and passing points.

THE FAR EAST

In China there was a similar tradition, although here the pergola was something of a hybrid including extended verandahs that adjoined the house or linked a series of buildings to genuine, free-standing examples set within a well ordered garden pattern. The Chinese were also genuinely fond of gates and archways of all descriptions, these often taking diverse forms, such as lotus petals, vases, shells and scabbard shapes. Trellis panels and complicated timber lattice work were woven into both screens and arches, many of which would look particularly handsome in virtually any garden today. Where the Chinese took great delight in training plants onto trellises, they kept their open

verandahs completely free from vegetation in an obvious effort to emphasize the purity of line. Some verandahs, although open at the sides, could be climbed by steps to a second walkway at a higher level, where the views both within and outside the garden would be altogether different.

Such subtleties were far beyond European gardeners of a similar period and although pergolas and arches showed a degree of eccentricity, they never showed such architectural grace and, apart from a few modern examples, are unlikely ever to do so.

As with arbours the pergola virtually disappeared in England with the arrival of the great landscape park, but it was not long before it blossomed once again with the Victorian villa garden of the 19th century.

The century opened with a new awareness of decorative gardening. Humphrey Repton, a genuinely gifted designer, took over the mantle worn so omnipotently by Brown. The former had far more time for the grounds that adjoined the house. Repton also used flower and ornament in a controlled manner which belied the excesses that were to come later in the century. He was fond of ironwork and freely used wrought iron arches to act as frames for the increasing range of plants that were being imported from all over the world. Wrought iron work, from the early nineteenth century has great adaptability, each piece being fashioned individually by a blacksmith. It can be and was, produced in delicate patterns that the later cast iron could not match. It is true that the Victorians had a predilection for grossness in style, certainly in the latter part of the century, but the materials they used often emphasized this.

CASTING AROUND

However, the very fact that casting produced a multiple product meant that the general public, rather than a privileged few, had access to a bewildering range of patterns, all

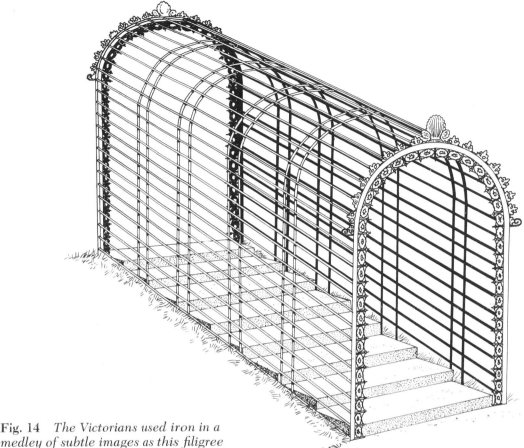

Fig. 14   *The Victorians used iron in a medley of subtle images as this filigree of rods and arches bears testimony.*

at a correspondingly reasonable price. A typical and unusual pergola is shown in Fig. 14. It is built over a flight of shallow steps and rises with the ground. This could be visually unsettling from the side elevation and would need careful counterbalancing with planting to prevent it looking as though it were sliding down the hill. In order to save money, only the first and last sections have been cast, the intermediate iron hoops, grouped in pairs, being left plain. Horizontal bars or wires give ample support for climbers, and such a bold statement looks almost as good plain as it would do planted. This is an important consideration for all pergolas and arches; foliage does much to mask or soften an unsatisfactory design which will be laid bare in winter for all to see.

Of course, iron was only one of the materials available; timber, stone, bricks, and even concrete, were all used at this time. Neither was their function purely decorative,

and in the kitchen garden a wide range of pergola-like tunnels were built to carry apples, pears and other fruits. Fruit, by its very nature, needs pruning and this makes it immensely adaptable to training. It also allows the crop to be gathered easily from paths positioned below or at the sides, all of which adds visual movement and enhances the decorative quality of the feature. There is a particularly splendid apple tunnel at Heale House in Wiltshire. The tunnel device was often taken to extremes with intricate pitched roofs and elaborate decoration. Such styles are rarely seen today, being largely eliminated by reason of cost, but they were fun!

We have already seen that towards the end of the century there was a revolution against the contorted but still popular flower garden, led largely by William Robinson who was joined by Gertrude Jekyll. While Robinson was essentially a plantsman, Jekyll fully understood the importance of architectural form which made her partnership with Lutyens so worth while. Lutyens had a brilliant eye for garden form and he used pergolas and overheads of all descriptions to control and frame views, as well as to draw together different parts of the overall scheme.

LUTYENS

One of his other great strengths, and one so often overlooked by architects of all periods, was his respect for local traditions and materials. This meant that house and garden attained a single unity, at one with the surrounding landscape.

A typical early work at Crooksbury House provided a south-facing fig court that linked two wings of the building. The robust pergola of brick and timber would look as good today as it did 90 years ago. The point is, however, that it was more than just a garden ornament, it was a positive element in pulling the two sections of building together. In short, it was an ideal link between house and garden, a precept that has always made sound sense.

The construction (Fig. 15a) is simple enough for any landscape gardener or competent house owner to tackle and consists of brick piers that start at ground level as 34 cm (13½ in) squares. The size decreases just over half way up to 23 cm (9 in), while the top two courses that act as pads to the timber framework are single bricks only. The point at which the piers reduce is precisely angled back and each is capped with a sawn brick, which was in all probability specially made for the job. The main beams that span the piers are very slightly curved, which gives a greater feeling of rhythm than straight timbers, while the intermediate lattice work, constructed from comparatively light

A pergola should always have a purpose, in this case a view of the well-positioned sundial. Note the contrasting climbers.

50

10 cm × 8 cm (4 in × 3 in) beams gives a strong feeling of perspective when viewed down the length of the pergola.

This is a simple pergola by Mr Lutyens' standards but it underlines the point so often ignored by today's designers and manufacturers that anything less substantial than this simply looks flimsy. It may take more work and use more material but in the long term, when clothed in climbing plants, it will repay the effort handsomely. Much of Lutyens' work was grand and sadly out of scale for today's confined plots, but his passion for gardens produced some quite outstanding designs, and the spirit of these can be freely imitated, provided one understands and accepts fundamental limitations.

But as well as playing a supporting role, pergolas were often set pieces. Typical of this is a fine example at Woodside, a country

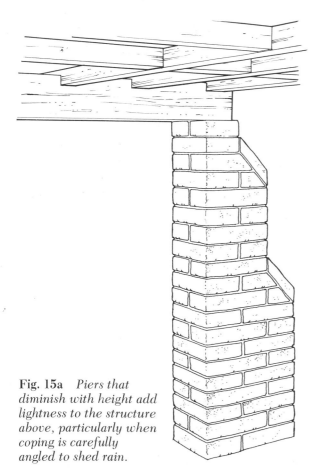

Fig. 15a *Piers that diminish with height add lightness to the structure above, particularly when coping is carefully angled to shed rain.*

house lying on gently falling ground at Chenies in Buckinghamshire. At the junction of two beautifully proportioned walks lies a small circular pool, over which is set a pergola resting on classic columns. The pool itself is tiny in a garden of such proportions, maybe 4.5 m (15 ft) across, but it is the pergola that draws the eye from a distance. The pool is seen only when one is comparatively near, creating a pleasurable surprise. It also has the effect of blocking the way so that one has to walk around it, naturally leading one towards the second main walk, set at right angles to the first.

The lesson to be learnt from this pergola is simple and slightly unusual, in that one cannot walk underneath it. It is quite simply a statement, a punctuation mark that tells you to stop, look and then move on in a different direction. Such a feature could make the ideal centrepiece to a much smaller formal garden and there are a number of manufacturers reproducing fine stonework at modest prices, most of which can be bought 'off the peg' and easily assembled. There are eight columns set in pairs on four bases, the massive oak beams that form the top giving the whole feature stability.

In complete contrast both in complexity and cost is an example built as a centrepiece, surrounding a well in the kitchen garden at 'Orchards', another country house at Godalming in Surrey. It should be remembered that kitchen gardens at the turn of this century were much more than allotments; they did indeed produce vegetables – although at 'Orchards' this function was undertaken in an adjoining garden – but they also produced fruit, herbs and a vast range of flowers both for cutting and as simple ornament. The feature is not a pergola but a series of four arches constructed from metal hoops. These are strapped onto tapered wooden posts which are, in turn, linked by light chains. The use of posts and chains was particularly popular at this time and made an ethereal framework that looks particularly good with rambling roses. Miss Jekyll in her wisdom makes a worthwhile and practical comment on this arrangement, suggesting that chains should be wound with well tarred cord so that shoots can be encouraged, and protected to some degree from the cold metal in winter. Alternatively, and altogether better, she suggests, 'is to have two chains, spread apart about 15 cm (6 in), with rigid iron ties, for training to this is more under control'. And in even more delightful prose 'All gardeners who have had to do with rose garlands know the trouble of the whole thing swinging around to the underside, like a saddle on a horse'. The transport may have changed, and tarred cord now impossible to get, but the commonsense of it all is refreshing.

Ropes between posts were also used and

Fig. 15b *These larch poles have been slotted into the stone piers, an unusual and attractive detail.*

this creates a slightly heavier and, I always think, 'nautical' feel. The ropes need renewing more often and if you do try it *do not* use the modern synthetic variety; it shines and looks totally out of place. Sometimes the hoops can be set alternately, one curving upward, the other down, and this can set up an interesting and altogether different rhythm.

Before leaving Lutyens' work, it is interesting to note that he rarely used rustic timbers in his pergolas. There are exceptions, but to my mind they clutter the essential clarity of line for which he is unique. One example which is both ingenious and unusual is shown in Fig. 15b.

Here he uses stone piers, but these could equally well be in brick, and near the top round spars of larch are set into the columns. This has the effect of producing an altogether different result which is visually very positive. This particular pergola was used on a sloping site and leads down in a series of rectangles, steps linking each pier and indicating a change of level.

Pergolas that step down with a slope are difficult to handle. Success lies in the generous steps, incorporating shallow risers in conjunction if possible with broad landings that lead away into terraces to either side. The construction should be simple, using local materials and straightforward timbers. If the 'pads' that bear the main timber cross pieces are carved or detailed sensitively, then a greater degree of 'life' is engendered. (Such attention is often lacking today and we are the poorer for it.)

PROPORTION

In fact, most pergolas look at their best on flat ground, in straight runs and, where space allows, of comfortable proportions. 2.25 m (7 ft 6 in) high is sensible and the width should be a little more, say between 2.5 m and 2.75 m (8 ft and 9 ft). As far as posts or piers are concerned, generally speaking these need to be between 2.75 m and 3.5 m (9 ft and 12 ft) apart.

An interesting example of a pergola that is too narrow for its height is shown in Fig. 16. The construction is good with brick piers, stone cappings and carefully worked, curved end timbers for emphasis. I particularly like the idea of trellis as a roof, although this would be a nightmare to replace once the climbers had established and rot set it. Unfortunately, the steps emphasize the inherent meanness of the path, and had these been wider it would have been a more comfortable entrance. The old cast iron pots are fun; they come out of the wash house boilers attached to any house more than 60 years old – I have one in my own garden which I removed while installing central heating! They are of ample size for most plants, and particularly climbers which need plenty of leg room. The only problem is drilling holes in the cast iron for drainage; it is a temperamental metal which tends to fight back.

Narrow pergolas make me feel distinctly uneasy, encouraging a brisk walk rather than a leisurely stroll. In complete contrast is

Fig. 16 *This traditional but slightly narrow pergola accelerates rather than slows feet, although the construction is quite superb.*

Opposite: *Here a framework of charming roses on a pergola enhances the view of the lawn*

Stone and timber appear almost indistinguishable owing to a delightful patina of age.

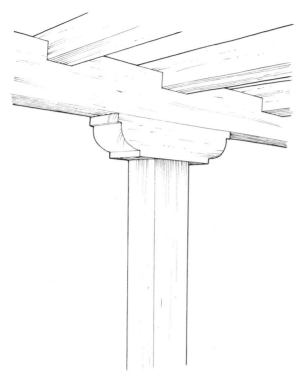

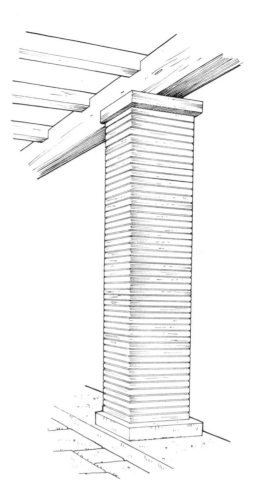

Fig. 17a *Timber pergolas are today so often stereotyped but 100 years ago the range of options was enormous. See how the pad at the top of the post is shaped and how carefully the beams have been notched in.*

Fig. 17b Right: *Tiles instead of bricks can build superb piers and when these are set off with solid timber and crisp stone, the results are well worth the effort.*

perhaps one of the best timber pergolas I have seen. The detailing is impeccable and I show this in the form of a working drawing (Fig. 17a). The width is ample for a generous path as well as planting on either side, with solid 15 cm × 15 cm (6 in × 6 in) posts rising from the latter. The longitudinal timbers rest on simple but very effective pads, while the cross braces are beautifully notched in directly above the uprights. This may all look obvious but it is in fact the garden designer at the peak of his craft. By virtue of being taken for granted, it succeeds very well indeed.

As a final glimpse of that golden and spacious age of gardening, look at the fine pergola that adjoins a racquet court at St. Clere, Kemsing. The piers are built from paving tiles (Fig. 17b) and the thinness of these helps provide a degree of lightness that would be impossible in brick or stone. Stone bases and caps work in contrast to the darker

tiles and the lowest base course of stone leads the eye down the entire length of the walk. At the top of the pergola a continuous, heavy beam echoes the line, while lighter cross members have been built into the wall on the other side. The only vulnerable point of this pergola is where the long stone step that carries the piers adjoins the lawn. Such an awkward upstand is always a headache for mowing and hand finishing is inevitable. Far better would be to run a course of brick or tiles adjoining the step and just below the turf so that a mower could run smoothly along without nudging the stone. A seasonal trim with an edging iron will keep things neat and crisp.

While gardens and their features 80 to 100 years ago are not always in scale with what we are accustomed to today, the lessons of good design, construction and suitability of purpose are equally as pertinent.

SMALLER GARDENS

Gardens are of course becoming smaller, which is the inevitable result of an increased urban awareness of the value of a 'backyard' and the impossible financial implications of running those glorious but labour intensive affairs of yesterday. It is also true that the percentage of home owners has increased, and it is natural that they take a greater personal interest in what is their own personal 'territory'. Many horticulturalists consider this trend to be retrogressive, feeling that plants are becoming relegated to ever smaller beds and their importance is correspondingly declining. While this may be true in as much that the available space is contracting, it does not follow that plants are becoming less important. From my own 20 years' experience of designing and building gardens, the value of plants is appreciated more than ever, and this same philosophy is shared by those who use my services. It is true that the cultivation of vegetables is not always practical, simply on the grounds of available space, but I must admit to finding the pursuit of ever larger and more perfect leeks, potatoes or onions particularly boring and tasteless, both in a culinary and aesthetic sense. The commercial grower is far better equipped to carry this out and as he becomes increasingly aware of the dangers of pesticides and herbicides, his product is ever more acceptable to an increasingly selective public.

On the other hand, the choice, range and general suitability of garden plants is rapidly expanding, and while some of these are indeed garish and do little to enhance their surroundings, the vast majority are quite the opposite. The explosion of specialist nurseries and well run garden centres bear ample testimony of this.

Along with the availability of plants is a vast selection of gardening hardware that includes paving, pots, pools and even pergolas that can be bought 'off the peg' and assembled at home. Pergolas of this kind are not always of the best design, but they provide a starting point and, when joined together and smothered with climbers, are more than acceptable. In addition to this, one enterprising chain is offering a collection of suitable plants to clothe the structure, taking much of the guesswork out of the entire operation. In the final analysis though, it all comes down to positioning and the best way to understand this is to look at a number of designs that use pergolas or arches.

As we have been talking of small gardens, the first example (Fig. 18) is of a real backyard, measuring 9 m × 5 m (30 ft × 17 ft). It belongs to two young professional people whose gardening time is limited because they both work in the catering business with its erratic hours. They wanted a garden that was easy to build, easy to run and, perhaps most important of all, easy on the eye. In physical terms the site was an uncompromising one, with a combination of dilapidated brick walls and tumble-down fences. The first job was to rectify these and at least make the garden secure. The only plants of any worth were a mature forsythia and an old apple tree in the bottom, right-hand corner. In addition, the back of the house faced north, meaning that sun, particularly in the early and late parts of the year, would strike only the bottom half of the garden. Add to all this the limited budget of a couple just married and things did not look too bright.

The first job in this and any other garden, is the initial organization of space and this fell into three broad areas. Moving away from the house, a relatively small but neat paved area was needed to give access to both the back door and the side passage that led away to the front of the house. A raised bed provided just a touch of vertical emphasis to the left-hand side and this was so positioned to balance the height and visual dominance of the arch. In this garden the arch is very important and carries out a number of functions. The first of these is space division: the arch separates the darker, utilitarian part of the garden from the softer, lighter and more

Opposite: *This is garden imagery on the grandest scale, trees leading the eye down to a strongly conceived viewing point.*

Here the pergola reaches its logical conclusion, completely buried beneath a torrent of bloom.

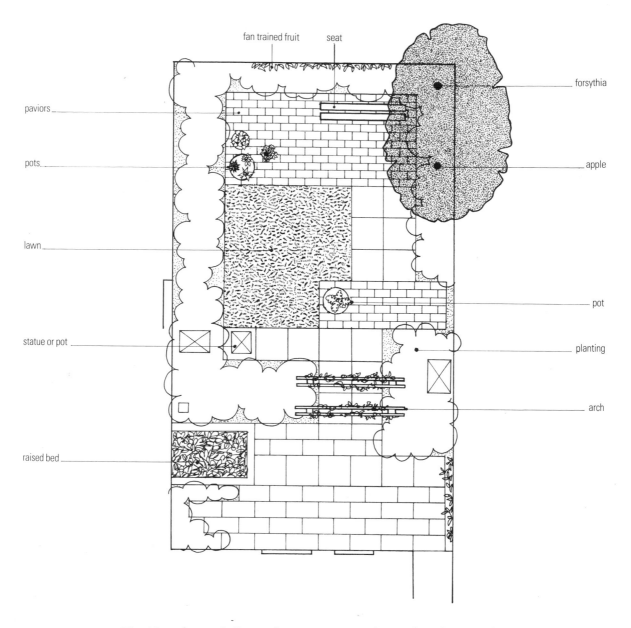

fan trained fruit

seat

forsythia

paviors

pots

apple

lawn

pot

statue or pot

planting

arch

raised bed

Fig. 18 *This arch forms the gateway into the garden, framing the view of the seat that acts as a focal point.*

decorative elements. Conversely, it is also a link bridging the two wings of planting and completing the envelope of soft foliage that surrounds the top of the garden. Where it is positioned, it also falls on the garden's 'golden section', that comfortable point approximately one-third along a given line that engenders a feeling of balance, and upon which most asymmetric designs are based. Of course this is more obvious from the plan or an upstairs window, but it feels undeniably correct when walking from end to end of the garden. At ground level the views are alto-

gether different and the arch is positioned exactly opposite the back door. When leaving this the eye is focused directly down the garden, pausing at the pot full of annual colour, then moving on finally to focus on the old cast iron and timber seat that acts as a classical, but undemonstrative, focal point. Incidentally, fill that pot carefully as too bright a colour will provide an overstatement and too pale would make it look anaemic. My own choice would be the delightful annual mimulus which with its clear yellow, is neither too brash nor bland.

In a relatively small garden the climbers for this arch need to be delicate rather than rampant and a good choice would be a dark purple, large-flowered clematis in conjunction with the netted gold leaves of the variegated Japanese honeysuckle, *Lonicera japonica* 'Aureo reticulata'. The latter is deliciously fragrant, which will be charming in such a tiny space.

The construction of the arch is very simple and this is important in a confined space. The uprights are of 10 cm × 10 cm (4 in × 4 in) square section, pressure-treated softwood. If possible try and make sure this is well seasoned as timber exposed to the elements for any period of time, particularly in our variable climate, can be subject to severe twisting and cracking. If you can go to the yard, ask a few pertinent questions and then if you can select your own, so much the better. The tops are 15 × 5 cm (6 × 2 in) and these neatly sandwich each pair of posts with additional, simple cross braces to hold the whole structure firm. The posts can be fixed into the ground in a number of ways, the most simple of which involves digging the holes, placing the posts in position and then backfilling with well rammed hardcore. A more durable result can be achieved with concrete, and this should be brought just proud of the surface and the shoulders sloped off to shed rain water and prevent it collecting. The vulnerable point for any post is just above ground level and a regular application of a non toxic preservative is advised every two years. Lastly, an increasingly popular method of fixing is to use metal sleeves. These are made to provide a snug fit for the post and are driven into the ground, making sure they are true. This is not always easy, as a buried stone can quite easily cause a frustrating deviation, but a more sophisticated type has screw adjustments that allow final realignment once the 'shoe' is firmly anchored. From experience, these devices may look quick and easy but they are relatively expensive, and a little extra time with sand and cement does the job equally well, although post renewal is more complicated. At all costs, never use those concrete spurs that are so popular for fences. On a boundary they are easily covered with planting but in the middle of the garden they are far too obvious.

Once under the arch, which naturally constricts the path, the garden takes on an altogether different dimension. The pot automatically pushes one across to the right, and the band of concrete paviors emphasizes the width of the plot, as do the courses of contrasting slabs closer to the house. Paths, only a single slab wide, can feel just a little too 'light' and here a double row 1.25 m (4 ft) across, leads onto the sunny sitting area that faces back towards the house. This too has been laid in paviors, an ideal material for the D.I.Y. gardener, requiring only simple bedding on sand which, in turn, is laid over a base of well compacted hardcore. A small lawn interlocks with the paving and planting to form an interesting composition and, although this would involve a degree of maintenance, its value in providing a softening influence is a definite bonus. It is also fair to point out that having paving on three sides of the grass acts as an ideal mowing edge, eliminating the chore of hand edging.

Planting wraps the garden about and softens the severe boundaries. Food production has not been entirely forgotten either, with the planting of a fan-trained peach or even nectarine on that warm, sunny, south facing fence.

USING DIAGONALS

Another small garden is shown in Fig. 19; the dimensions are virtually the same 9 m × 6 m (30 ft × 20 ft), but the treatment is quite different. This was a garden I recently designed for the popular BBC *Gardeners' World* programme. It was built at Barnsdale and we subsequently answered over 4000 enquiries from interested viewers. In this scheme the whole pattern is turned at 45° to the bound-

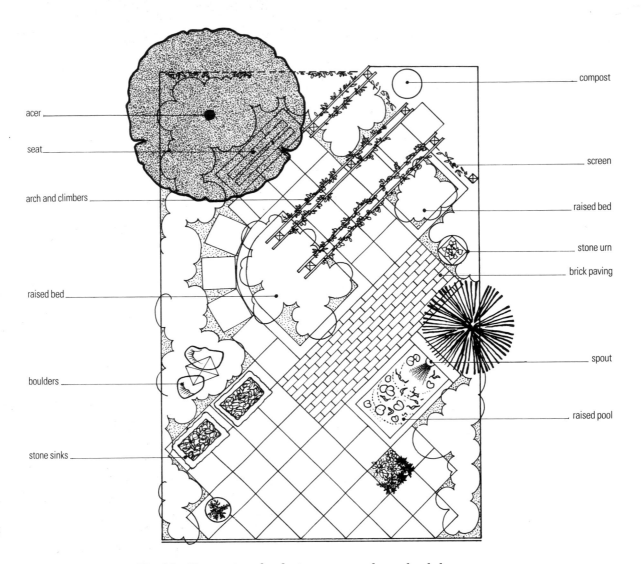

acer

seat

arch and climbers

raised bed

boulders

stone sinks

compost

screen

raised bed

stone urn

brick paving

spout

raised pool

Fig. 19 *By turning the design at an angle we lead the eye away from rectangular boundaries. The arch spans the planted areas providing unity and vertical emphasis.*

aries and this immediately turns the eye away from the severe rectangle formed by the fences. The design was, in fact, built up over a number of phases and this, a garden for a retired couple, was the culmination. The house would naturally be at the bottom of the page, the terrace area of 0.5 m × 0.5 m (2 ft × 2 ft) Cotswold colour precast slabs, opening out from French windows or sliding doors. To the right, a small pool fitted with a submersible pump and spout sets up delightful reflections on a hot summer's day. In the centre of the garden, acting as both a pivot and balance to the pool, is situated a raised bed, this being home for either salad crops or mixed planting. Paths swing around this cen-

tral feature and the extended arch spans the section of paving that leads up to the seat. Such an arch is something of a hybrid, partly the former but at the same time almost a pergola, as it extends over the path that leads through to the neat area allocated for compost and the inevitable garden clutter. Its construction is similar to the arch we considered in the last garden, except that the span is greater, which necessitates three sets of posts instead of two. It also has a stronger design element, emphasizing the diagonal

The art of pleaching is both subtle and effective, forming a vegetative pergola. Notice this walk has really nowhere to go!

line of the garden and tying this back into the boundaries to produce a coherent overall concept. This is a garden full of interest and because one can walk right around it, the feeling of space is increased, together with an awareness of levels with the raised beds and pergola beams.

From these two small compositions it becomes increasingly obvious that you cannot take garden features in isolation. If you are going to use an arch or pergola, then its location will bear very heavily on the whole design and not just part of it.

COTTAGE GARDENS

Moving up the scale many people consider cottage gardens to be a typically English institution. What they are usually thinking of are the idealized paintings or photographs on the front of chocolate boxes. The real article was very different, often built up from a fruitful vegetable plot, a sprinkling of free range chickens and a couple of goats, the by-products of which kept everybody in good heart. Flowers there may have been, but these were more often than not relegated to a small area by the house rather than the expansive schemes so often pictured.

I recently had the opportunity to plan the gardens of a fine old farmhouse in Buckinghamshire. These were set around a magnificent range of buildings and the most intimate space occupied the old farmyard, adjoined by the farmhouse on one side, a row of pigsties on another, with barns and stone walls completing the picture. A new rear entrance was formed and a path ran between two barns to reach the backdoor (Fig. 20).

The brief was for a 'cottage style' garden, utilizing as many materials as possible found on site and salvaged from the renovation works. A pergola was considered essential, as was a sundial, chamomile lawn and old-fashioned, fragrant plants. The whole area which faced south was sheltered by high

stone walls and was, in short, a gardener's paradise.

The whole design is based on a series of interlocking rectangles and while many people might consider this a severe approach, it is traditional and, when softened by planting, can be extraordinarily restful. The first job, after clearing the site of rubble and 300 years of rubbish, was to convert the pigsties into an east-facing loggia. This was achieved by lifting and rebuilding the old tiled roof, and the long line of this building set the main theme of the garden. Paving in old York stone gave access to the gate, the path passing under a simple, timber arch, covered by the delicate blue *Clematis macropetala*. Aromatics, lavender and raised beds flank the path, with solid stone steps leading up to the backdoor. The view looking back is a joy, the ample paved area with sprawling plants set in the joints, gives onto the pergola that really forms the backbone of the whole garden. Old brick piers rise from the planting on either side and the pergola top is formed from massive old oak beams that were found too weak for service within the building. The beams were not cleaned up drastically or shaped, their solid, slightly irregular outline acting in unison with the surrounding buildings, some of which were half-timbered themselves. The pathway below takes the form of stepping stones through low-growing, ground cover plants. As an intermediate focal point the sundial is just right. It, too, is constructed from stone and it slows one down before passing through the high yew hedge that is carefully positioned level with the end of the sties.

This arch focuses attention across the top lawn towards the gate that was newly formed in the old wall. This is not primarily intended for access but it does provide a tantalizing view for a distance of nearly fifteen miles across gently falling farmland. It should always be remembered that such a vision of space enormously increases the apparent size of the immediate garden; and the high hedge provides not only space division within the

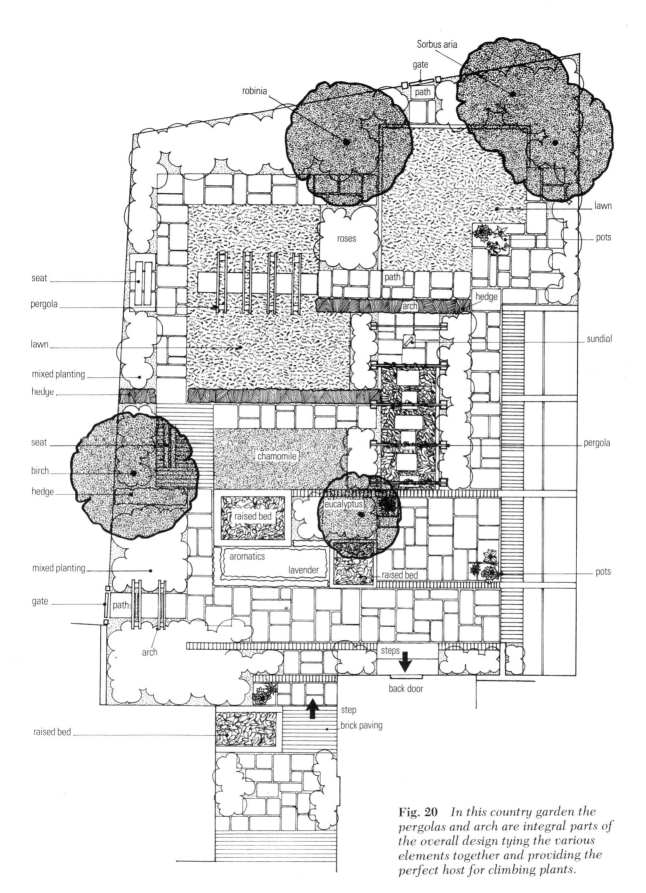

Sorbus aria

robinia

gate
path

seat

pergola

lawn

mixed planting

hedge

seat

birch

hedge

mixed planting

gate

path

arch

raised bed

roses

path

arch

hedge

chamomile

raised bed

aromatics

lavender

eucalyptus

raised bed

lawn

pots

sundial

pergola

pots

steps

back door

step

brick paving

Fig. 20 *In this country garden the pergolas and arch are integral parts of the overall design tying the various elements together and providing the perfect host for climbing plants.*

65

design, but it shields the second pergola that runs at right angles to the first and takes one across the slightly larger lawn. It terminates at the arbour and fine old timber seat that is one of a pair, its counterpart facing the fragrant chamomile lawn.

Planting is woven throughout this garden, producing subdivision, colour, fragrance and, above all, a charisma of old English summers that takes us back to a time when life was measured by a more leisurely beat.

Opposite: *In this delightfully pleached avenue a climax is provided by the swathe of sunlight across the lawn, an element all too often neglected in our temperate climate.*

IN FRONT OF THE HOUSE

In a similar mood, but in a different situation, the next illustration is indeed a cottage but the front approach rather than the rear garden. Now here is something that has changed in the last 50 years: cars, as opposed to pedestrians or even horses, take up more room and provide near visual disaster in many a garden. The point is you have to be practical about vehicles. It may *look* best to relegate them to an area to the side or some distance from the house; in the summer, a pleasant saunter to the front door is fine. However, in the rain and gales a few months later it is simply not on, and the shorter the

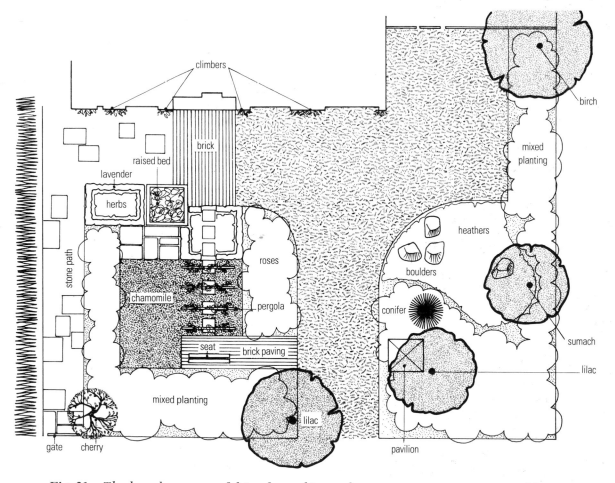

Fig. 21 *The broad expanse of drive for parking and garage access are counteracted here by a strong design incorporating both pavilion and pergola.*

dash for cover the better. This means that drivers and their cars need to be close to the front door. Now both these elements are dominant, cars being bright and flashy, drives large and dull – it is little wonder that many front gardens, or what is left of them, are completely swamped in the process. The problem is basically one of scale, and any area planned with cars in mind must not only cater for ease of access but find some way of redressing the visual balance. To try and do this with planting and features at ground level will go only part of the way to finding an answer; what we really need is a degree of vertical emphasis. Trees, although useful, are not always the answer because some species produce a sticky sap, others cast too much shade in a relatively small area and most produce masses of leaves that need sweeping up in autumn. However, pergolas and overhead structures can be ideal, not only giving emphasis where needed, but extending an architectural line out into the garden, providing a natural link with the house.

This first example is indeed a cottage and you can see that the drive takes up nearly half of the total area (Fig. 21). Initially, the drive surface is vitally important and here gravel is ideal, blending with black half timbering and ochre colour-washed walls. The garage is to the side of the house and, as well as providing access to this, the drive sweeps up to the front door. At this point the broad band of brick paving indicates a basic change of use between wheels and feet, and it also changes the whole emphasis of the garden plan. Standing by the door, looking away from the house, one's view is immediately drawn across the herb bed and under the pergola, terminating at the seat that acts as a natural focal point. As well as stepping-stones which link the two areas of brick paving, the section under the seat extends across the drive, reminding motorists to slow down and leading the eye across to the pavilion, a very prettily disguised oil tank.

The remaining part of the garden is given over to a strong architectural pattern of plant-ing, chamomile and paving which, although distinctly traditional, does by its strength of line provide a very effective counterbalance to the drive.

The pergola itself is of simple timber construction, once again using 10 cm × 10 cm (4 in × 4 in) posts sandwiched by 15 cm × 5 cm (6 in × 2 in) cross members. Planting is vital to increase the drama, and here I chose that giant of vines, *Vitis coignetiae* (Japanese crimson glory vine), with its huge leaves that turn to a splendid, ruddy bronze in autumn. Such a vigorous plant enjoys regular feeding and an annual dose of good organic manure, lightly forked in around the roots in the dormant winter months, is absolutely ideal.

CAR PORTS

Along with the ubiquitous motor car has come a plague of unsightly, prefabricated garages. Perhaps even worse is the car port, a distant relative to the pergola but usually distorted out of all recognition. This is a pity because there is a definite possibility here of creating something worth while.

In many a front garden situation, the garage sits uncomfortably to one side of the plot, often an afterthought and definitely out of architectural step with the house. In the gap there is usually ample room for a carport and this space frequently gives access to the back and side doors. In order to link garage, carport and house, a pergola can be run from the former to a point just short of the first house window. To make an effective bridge it is important not to stop the pergola on the corner of the building, always a weak design point, but to carry it on as far as possible without creating shadow problems through the windows. To reinforce this line at ground level a broad band of brick paving could be run from a point on the far side of the front door, right across the face of the house and drive, to terminate at the same point as the pergola on the far side of the garage. If the remaining garden area is also handled firmly, this will have the effect of leading the eye away from a haphazard garage.

As far as this pergola construction is concerned, it needs to be very positive and planed 23 cm × 5 cm (9 in × 2 in) beams are ideal. These are supported by black metal poles and the brickwork was painted white or a colour to match other parts of the building. As the front elevation is in full sun why not plant the pergola with just one species, the remarkable deciduous climber *Actinidia kolomikta* (Kolomikta vine). This is one of my favourite plants, a twisting climber that has heart-shaped leaves splashed with pink and cream; it looks for all the world as though someone has thrown a bucketful of paint over it. The flower is insignificant and it loses its leaves relatively early in autumn – but throughout summer it is nothing short of magic. Neither is it fussy about soil; I have one growing by my back door in a quite minimal depth of soil and surrounded by paving.

As a final example of front garden design incorporating arches look at Fig. 22. This is a completely asymmetric composition for an awkwardly narrow plot that runs across the face of the house. The drive in this case is neatly disposed of to one side and in this situation it would be impossible because of limited space to turn in as far as the front door. This allows ample scope for a series of interlocking rectangles of brick and precast paving that form an attractive pathway. To link house and garden a pair of arches span the path and there is no doubt that these heighten the drama of what is, after all, a straightforward route. It is sensible to bear in mind that where an arch or pergola spans a busy walkway, then the climbers that clothe it should not be too vigorous. If they are, they need constant attention to keep them in check and consequently never look at their best. They also tend to produce all their flower at the top, which is of little benefit as a view except from a bedroom window.

An ideal choice would be a combination of the early and late flowering clematis. Of the first, 'Barbara Jackman' and 'Mrs. Cholmondeley' are ideal, with a long flowering seasons, while from the latter group try any of

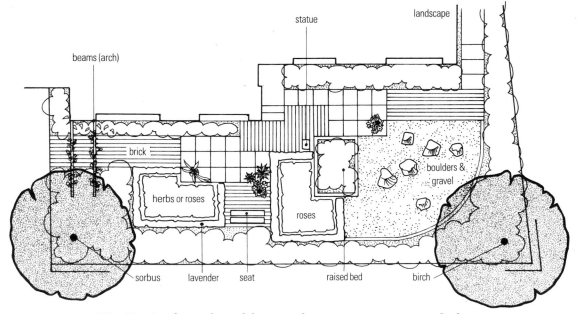

Fig. 22 *In this awkward front garden a contemporary interlocking design acts as the perfect foil to crisp architecture, the overhead beams framing the path to the front door.*

the Jackmanii hybrids. These could include 'Ernest Markham', 'Jackmanii Superba' or 'Perle d'Azure'.

In this situation the clematis could be grown in pairs, one from the bed adjoining the house and one trained up the metal supports, though do remember that any bed close to a house needs additional irrigation, owing to overhanging eaves and the possible 'rain shadow' caused by the house.

FLOORING MATERIALS

Not only does the position and direction of a pergola or arch determine movement through it, but so too does the shape and construction of the feature itself. Length is obviously important, taking into account that an arch is a transient affair while a long pergola is a tunnel with a defined beginning and end. Added to this is the type of paving and the way in which it is laid. This can make a great difference to how quickly feet and eye reach the other end.

In our country garden the route was by stepping-stones through ground cover and this naturally slows one down, as you have to make a positive, but pleasurable effort to pick a way from one stone to another. In direct contrast would be brick paving, laid on edge in stretcher bond, with the courses running up and down the pergola. This is a visual racetrack and if there is a focal point at either end much of the enjoyment of a leisurely walk is lost in a subconscious effort to reach the finale. Brick paving laid across the path has the opposite effect, slowing things down. In other words different paving materials, have a different character and influence on the eventual position in which they are laid. Smooth crisp paving is also an accelerator, while cobbles that provide a slightly uneven

The laburnum pergola at Barnsley House. Even out of season it retains both charm and a strong directional emphasis.

70

surface are quite the opposite. In the classic Laburnum Walk at Barnsley House in Gloucestershire (p. 71) the paving is an interesting visual compromise. The cobbles, laid in a variety of patterns and panels, do indeed induce lethargy, but the strongly linear framework on either side has the opposite effect. All in all these cancel themselves out, but for my own taste it is a little too 'busy'. What you have to remember is that the pergola and planting set the keynote and, as such, the other elements in the design should be subservient. The Barnsley pergola also illustrates a number of other points. It is primarily planted with laburnum, which in itself is slightly unusual as it is more often found as a small free standing garden tree. The beauty of its drooping blossom does, however, make it an ideal specimen and the effect of 'golden rain' when in full bloom is stunning.

Laburnum in the open is often just a little brash, but when the flower is seen in the subdued light of a pergola it is toned down to a very acceptable level. The pergola supports are of very simple thin iron, welded into hoops and have, over the years, become almost invisible. This is of course exactly right as it is the plant, and not the supporting structure, that is important. In fact the Laburnum stems have become the main framework. Among these have been planted a number of Wisteria and although these are still young, their blossom sets up an extended flowering pattern slightly earlier in the season. The simple stone column at the end of the walk is effectively set against a dark background and is emphasized even more by the fact that it lies in sunlight.

Focal points do have their merit at the end of such a walk but the most effective pergola I have seen did just the opposite. It was built

Fig. 23 *Hooped timber arches are stunningly integrated to form a superb pergola. Wires are stretched along the top to carry climbing plants, forming a tunnel of soft foliage.*

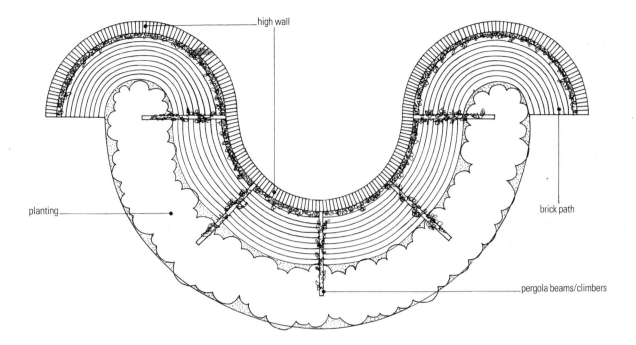

high wall

planting

brick path

pergola beams/climbers

Fig. 24 *This serpentine wall is echoed by the brick path at ground level. Pergola beams extend over the path, the supports rising from the strongly shaped border.*

within a large country garden set on the edge of an escarpment that overlooked the Cotswolds. The pergola was so designed that one entered it at an oblique angle from the intimacy of a largely enclosed composition. Once within the walk all the dimensions changed as the far end simply disappeared into space. The whole structure had been designed right on the edge of the scarp and as one walked down it the view unfolded into a breathtaking panorama. At the end a series of broad steps dropped away to a sunken viewing platform, quite invisible from the beginning of the pergola but a point of high drama in the overall design. The view from this pergola changed throughout the year, as did the light values from dawn to dusk. This kind of touch lifts a garden from simple competence to sheer genius, but it happens very rarely.

So we can see that pergolas fall into two main divisions, those that are subservient to the plants they bear or the view they encompass, and those that are built to a specific pattern that sets up its own rhythm.

IN THEIR OWN RIGHT

The pergola shown in Fig. 23 is a perfect example of the latter. It is not a home-built job and it would need the services of a skilled carpenter, being constructed from a series of hooped arches, each one securely fastened to the next. Along the top, galvanized wires form an almost invisible support for climbing plants. The hoops form both the sides of the pergola as well as the top and this is one situation, as far as I am concerned, where planting can play second fiddle. This sort of feature becomes a vital structural element within the garden framework and to smother it with climbers would be entirely detrimental.

A similarly architectural pergola is shown in Fig. 24 but this one has a quite different purpose. Here we have a long, south-facing wall which has been subdivided into a series of semi-circular bays, alternately playing host to a sitting area and pergola. Such a strong

Opposite: *These stepping stones are critical in slowing one's progress to a saunter towards the distant white seat. The planting is aptly English with roses gently arching over metal hoops.*

Scaffold poles and sawn-down railway sleepers form an undemonstrative frame for the rampant Russian vine, Polygonum baldschuanicum. *Gravel and paving provide a no nonsense floor.*

shape obviously sets up a very positive rhythm and this has been accentuated by the pergola that runs off the wall. The paving pattern naturally leads one through this space and the dappled shade cast by the overhead beams is a refreshing contrast from a real suntrap situation. The climbing plants used here are slightly unusual, being suitable for a semi-mediterranean climate that is to be found in the far west, virtually frost-free parts of the British Isles.

Another classic English pergola is shown on p. 74. This too is constructed from a series of hoops, but this time in iron. It is interesting to see just how different in appearance the much lighter iron supports are. The paving shows an interesting use of line, the staggered stepping stones emphatically widening the path and producing a slight stutter that slows one down on the way towards the seat, again set effectively against a dark background.

Planting here is of pink and white roses, a delightful combination that links perfectly with the grey cotton lavender that grows through the gravel at ground level.

Gravel is again used alongside the modern pergola shown above. This is a strongly geometric little garden that cleverly exploits the slight change in level with a series of raised beds and steps. The raised beds are in fact built from railway sleepers, these giving the design a strong horizontal line. The pergola is also constructed from sleepers, sawn down the middle and set on top of steel poles, which have been painted a matt black to match in colour. The climber in this case is Russian vine, *Polygonum baldschuanicum* (knotweed) and, while many people consider it a rampant pest, it really is a fabulous plant. It is undeniably vigorous but can be kept in check with a pair of shears. The white flowers, though individually small, are freely borne in panicles throughout the summer and autumn. Where quick cover is needed it is hard to beat – excellent for oil tanks and garages!

OVER WATER

Pergolas and water do not at first seem a likely combination but there is nothing more fascinating or unexpected than a bridge covered with a framework of flower and foliage. Water is always attractive and a bridge naturally heightens the drama. This is increased by a tunnel, provided that there is a suitable handrail over which one can lean and watch the reflections. A classic example is at Monet's garden in Giverny, France. This forms a graceful arch which is emphasized by slender poles and echoed by delicate toprails. These play host for wisteria, the pale blue flowers blending with the turquoise bridge, an unusual but nevertheless attractive colour combination.

Audley End in Essex is another example, although altogether different in style. This is a flat span, built in timber with simple wooden boards that provide a suitable deck. Both railings and hoops that arch over the bridge are iron, with wires to carry climbing roses. As well as being a positive statement in its own right, this pergola links two quite different parts of the gardens, one dark woodland, the other formal garden, providing excellent drama.

Although we have considered shrubs, hardy perennials and climbers throughout this book, it is fair to say that for the latter pergolas are ideal. Here a climber can experience the best possible growing conditions with light, air and ample natural irrigation available from all quarters. Climbers or shrubs grown against a wall or screen often encounter problems directly associated with inadequate soil and water. There is also the problem with some of the more rampant and thick-skinned kinds such as *Magnolia grandi-*

flora, or an ancient wisteria that can damage the structure that supports them. Wisteria can certainly badly distort ironwork over a period of years and nearly any climber, when left unchecked, can quickly run up and under the eaves, penetrating a roof space and allowing the ingress of damp.

The basic requirements of suitable soil, good preparation and aftercare are imperative if any plant is to give of its best. It is also wise, particularly if pergolas are built on substantial foundations, to plant the climber a short distance from the bottom of the post or column, angling it back and tying it in accordingly. Always make sure that wires and supports are both sufficient *and* neatly positioned. There is no quicker way to ruin a carefully built structure than covering it with assorted oddments of twine or wires.

WHICH CLIMBER?

Many of the examples of pergolas we have looked at have been covered with roses, but choosing these for best effect is not always easy. There are two basic types: climbers and ramblers. The latter are historically the older of the two, being with us for well over 100 years. They are extremely vigorous as a group, with long stems bearing masses of comparatively small flowers. When in flower they are usually a mass of colour but it is a one off show as ramblers are not repeat flowering. They also tend to be victims of the old plague of mildew which necessitates constant spraying if they are to look their best. Pruning is essential as flowers are carried on the new wood, and to look handsome on a pergola the long stems need constant tying in. There is a lot of work with a rambler and while this was, of necessity, acceptable in Miss Jekyll's day, it certainly provides a headache today. Climbers are far more amenable, flowering on old wood over a longer period. This means that once a framework is built up, which can be trained right around a pergola or arch, then

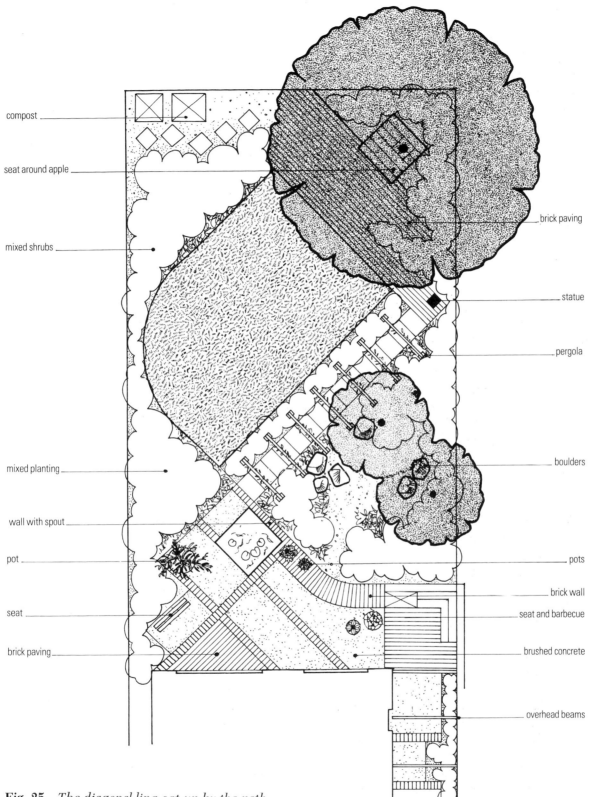

compost

seat around apple

mixed shrubs

mixed planting

wall with spout

pot

seat

brick paving

brick paving

statue

pergola

boulders

pots

brick wall

seat and barbecue

brushed concrete

overhead beams

Fig. 25 *The diagonal line set up by the path and pergola terminates at the statue, a necessary focal point near the top of the garden. Such a long pergola creates dappled shade and attractive views to either side.*

flowers can be expected at virtually all points. The range of plants is now enormous and a few hours studying a specialist book will mean that you get exactly what you want.

Apart from roses, the choice of climbers is enormous and we have already mentioned many excellent examples. However, one or two of my own rather unusual favourites would make a useful addition.

We have used *Actinidia kolomikta* (Kolomikta vine) but try the Chinese gooseberry, *Actinidia chinensis*, in its variegated form with cream and yellow leaves. *Aristolochia macrophylla (A. durior)* is nicknamed Dutchman's pipe. The leaves are heart-shaped but the flowers are extraordinary, tubular and bent into a syphon at the bottom. The colour too is subtle, a combination of yellowish-green with a green and purple-brown mouth. The common hop, *Humulus lupulus* is a lot of fun, and vigorous too. In full sun grow the golden variety 'Aureus' with its soft yellow leaves. No garden is complete without a jasmine and most of us are familiar with the fragrant summer flowering *Jasminum officinale* (common white jasmine) but, if space permits grow the gorgeous *Jasminum × stephanense*. It is in fact the only known hybrid, with fragrant pale pink flowers appearing in June and July. Finally, an unusual climber, which has the disadvantage of poisonous milky juice when damaged, is *Periploca graeca* (silk vine). It is vigorous, with delightful flowers over an inch across, green outside and browny-purple within. It has a not unpleasant perfume and is useful later in the season, flowering in July and August. The seeds are a bonus, being borne in pairs nearly 15 cm (6 in) long.

But although climbers bring a pergola alive, and although they are vital to its existence, it is the structure itself that is of greatest importance, at least in the criteria that I set as a designer. If we return to this as a final statement it will reinforce the importance of the basic concept.

In Fig. 25 I have shown a modern garden of reasonable size but rectangular in shape. Like our tiny design for the BBC, I have turned the whole pattern at an angle to the house and boundaries. The main terrace is constructed of 'brushed' concrete and panels of brick paving, a low brick wall acting as a broad seat by the pool. From this point a path leads diagonally away between the alpine and scree garden on the right and lawn on the left. Such a diagonal line opens up the garden along its longest dimension, increasing available space. To reinforce this the pergola spans the path, framing both the view of the statue and providing a soft glimpse of lawn. All this adds depth to the overall composition, dividing the garden and also providing a delightful view back towards the house from the brick-paved sitting area at the top of the garden.

This overhead collection of beams and timbers, then, is as pertinent now as it was in its viniferous days over 5000 years ago. The construction has changed little, but the setting could be in a different world from those walled Egyptian gardens of the Nile Delta. Perhaps this simply reinforces the adage of there being very few new ideas in gardening. It would seem that the pergola is here to stay.

4

Gazebos

A ROOM WITH A VIEW

Garden buildings have, since the very earliest times, been an essential part of many compositions. However, in most instances such buildings had a specific purpose, which was very often symbolic or religious. In the Mediterranean, where civilization flowered, living outside was, if not a necessity, at least popular for the obvious advantages of a cool breeze and lower temperatures. But while bedrooms, dining rooms, aviaries, grottoes and all kinds of other buildings flourished, the gazebo had, and still does have, one sole purpose, and that purpose is emphatic: it *must* encompass a view. It can of course be argued that any room, pavilion or structure within a garden has a view, but the gazebo's job is not mundane: its view should, if not specific, be of sufficient importance for its creation. In other words the 'essential' gazebo is not primarily an ornament (although it may have incidentally become one), it is a viewing platform.

Some of the earliest buildings of this type date from approximately the third century AD and were born out of the Taoist religion that then flourished in China. This embraced the principles of a retreat into nature, where man could be at one with the environment and thus release himself from the cares and pressures that are inseparable from an advanced civilization. Such philosophy is recurrent in all cultures, and at all times in history to the present day. In China gardens and nature are synonymous and from that time pavilions, which fulfilled the same function as a gazebo, were built to view it. Such pavilions later became heavily embellished with splendid curving roofs that soared with fantastic and beautiful rhythms. The Chinese also have a great fondness for colour and there is none of the inhibition seen in Western garden design. Garden buildings have glazed roof tiles, painted columns and decorated railings. All of this is in direct contrast to the 'natural' garden landscape and looks the better for it.

In Japan the concept is rather different, and although gardens are built to represent elements in the landscape they are far more stylized. Each rock, stepping-stone, plant and tree is positioned precisely, and as early as the eleventh century there was a code of practice that set these elaborate paramaters. With the introduction of the tea ceremony, pavilions were an essential part of the garden, but the role of these was meditative and their purpose was not only to view the garden in which they were constructed.

The Moguls built and enjoyed gardens of great beauty throughout India. Water is an essential ingredient and many fine examples can still be seen today. While cascades, pools and canals provide relief from the oppressive heat, so too does shade. Garden buildings and pavilions are ingenious and handsome and many of the latter are sited in or over water for obvious reasons. In Kashmir, where the plains have a superb backdrop of mountains, pavilions were built to take advantage of the views, thus providing a genuine link with the later gazebo of western Europe.

But the latter was a very different place in medieval times. Here the dark ages turned architecture towards fortification, and what gardens there were lay enclosed within monastery walls. Garden buildings were not common and it was not until the fourteenth century that pavilions started to appear in English gardens. Sometimes these were placed on top of mounts, the latter often being recorded in gardens of this period. The mount may well have been handed down as a relic of the raised ground on which the castle or fortified house had stood at an earlier date, and because the gardens were still enclosed such raised pavilions would have a clear view of the country beyond which was not possible at ground level.

Both the Italian and French Renaissance produced gardens the like of which had never been seen before – and in all probability will never be seen again. Their scale was enormous and their order complete. Water provided the dominant element in both countries and their strength of purpose did not include the smaller elements of garden design of which the pavilion is an example. There are always exceptions of course, and with the use of treillage, such designers as Le Nôtre, the most famous French garden architect, did construct buildings. However, these were usually enormous and more to do with the parade of court finery than the contemplation of a view.

With the passing of Louis XIV, the sun king, gardens that were totally and rigidly ordered were overtaken by a genuine feeling of relief. A basic degree of geometry remained but this was increasingly tempered with additions of a diverse nature, of which the 'Jardin Anglo-Chinois' was one. Here the pavilion reappeared, along with bridges, grottoes and meandering paths. The original philosophy of these was never understood in its new setting and the whole composition was really a series of unrelated focal points. The views from the pavilion would have been equally confusing.

In England the need for change never seemed as urgent as it did on the Continent, the Channel saving us from a cultural invasion as it has done so many times militarily speaking. Tudor gardens under Henry VIII and Elizabeth were still medieval in both form and outlook, evolving only very slowly. Unfortunately many were then swept away in the frenzied 'improvements' of William Kent and, more drastically, by 'Capability' Brown. One of the most charming to survive in virtually its original form is Montacute in Somerset. The house was built quickly and solidly but successive generations never had

sufficient capital to carry out the modernizations practised by so many other landowners. As a result Montacute stayed in a delightful state of suspended animation, along with its grounds and gardens. To this day, the latter are kept impeccably, at present being managed by the National Trust. The plan is basically rectilinear with broad paths that give access to lawns and planting. The corners of the garden are defined by the most exquisite gazebos, raised above the general level and built in stone. Not only do they act as punctuation marks in the overall design, they also command fine views both in and out of the garden. Montacute in high summer is an unforgettable experience with planting in borders that ramp gently up to fine stone walls and frame the gazebos.

AWAY FROM FORMALITY

In the later landscape gardens, buildings were used far more as focal points than viewpoints, although the park does indeed unfold as one moves from temple to obelisk. These buildings were for all to see and were consequently often of considerable size and complexity.

It was not until the nineteenth century that there was a real explosion of gardens and the ornamentation with which to fill them. Of this ornamentation buildings played a large part mimicking styles from all over the world. There were cottages from Bengal, China, and Timbuktu, while closer to home buildings were said to be of Scottish or Welsh influence, although it is difficult to understand exactly how these could look different – it was obviously all in the eye of the beholder! Virtually all of these were in timber, with an assortment of thatched, shingled or slated roofs, and because of an inherent tendency to rot very few have survived, although a browse through any catalogue of the period is fascinating.

The point was really that gardening, at

least as far as any recognizable theme was concerned, had lost its way. Styles were numerous, the choice and availability almost unlimited. It was not surprising, therefore, that the resulting designs were a compromise, gathering ideas from the previous 2000 years and working them into a pattern that suited each individual owner, but at least this in itself was a step forward as there were no longer any rigid criteria that had to be adhered to in the name of fashion. Another ingredient also became increasingly important, which was simply a sense of humour.

Many of the grand gardens of the past had whimsical owners, and water in particular was used in unexpected and sometimes socially devastating ways. Jets would burst forth from seats; statues would relieve themselves at guests; and ladies' crinolines were particularly prone to the aquatic japes of an unrelenting host. All this, however, was expensive and often necessitated complicated one-off constructional work. The Industrial Revolution changed all that and the market was flooded with outrageous mimicry from every age, country and fertile imagination that was able to create a suitable (or unsuitable) garden product. At last the forerunner of the ubiquitous garden gnome was born, something that has caused more controversy than almost any other subject during the past 100 years.

Of course, during the nineteenth century there were those gardens that were restrained and, as the nineties drew to a close, there was an increasing awareness and desire for a more coherent style in all areas of design, from textiles to gardens. In some of the larger gardens the owners still looked back to the reassurance of Renaissance Italy but this dependence was becoming less as genuine confidence took over. On the whole there was still a classical flavour, but Sir Edwin Lutyens was interpreting this in a thoroughly vernacular style. His gardens – and for his superb buildings alone he was almost undoubtedly the best garden designer of his day – evoked an altogether new and perfectly English style. Miss Jekyll and others gave life to the framework but it was Lutyens' underlying pattern that was important. Out of those patterns some of the most delightful and unique garden buildings and gazebos were born.

THE THUNDER HOUSE

Lutyens of course designed Miss Jekyll's own house and also part of the gardens at Munstead Wood in West Surrey. This was not an easy project as the gardens had in fact been started some years before and the position of the main building had to be planned accordingly. Lutyens' hand in the garden plan is not so obvious and, as one would expect, planting, grass walks and a soft backdrop of trees set the overall theme. There is certainly a terrace, a pergola and a number of carefully sited sitting areas. There is also a fine but simple gazebo. I say fine because, unlike so many others, it is essentially a plain little building, constructed from local stone to match that used elsewhere in the house and garden. The philosophy of the place is described perfectly in Miss Jekyll's own words:

'At the far end of the Kitchen garden, where the north and west walls join at an uneven angle, stands a little building – a raised gazebo. From inside the garden its floor level is gained by a flight of steps that wind up with one or two turns. Its purpose is partly to give a fitting finish to a bare looking piece of wall, and partly to provide a lookout place over the fields and the distant range of chalk hills to the north; for the region of the house and garden is so much encompassed by woodland that there is no view to the open country. The little place is most often used when there is thunder about, for watching the progress of the storm, and an incised stone on the garden side bears its name of "Thunder House".'

It should of course be remembered that Munstead Wood was not a large garden when measured against its contemporaries, but it is when looked at in the light of today's re-

This classic gazebo at Montacute House is utterly charming with a soaring roof that emphasizes the corner point of the garden. The planting is subtly graded in height and texture.

Opposite: *Modern gazebos can still be constructed from traditional materials. Reconstituted stone piers and balustrade are the perfect foil for modern paving and walling.*

stricted surroundings. At that time a gazebo
might serve a number of purposes, the visual
aspect being only one of them. It was considered an 'outpost', an escape from the more
rigid architecture and etiquette of the main
house. It thus became a withdrawing room, a
study, or a place to take tea, and so on.
Depending on its proximity to the house, its
style was more or less in keeping, although
the basic constructional materials were usually of a type. If close enough it might be
linked back to the house by a pergola and if
the former were half timbered, then so too
should be the gazebo. Changes in level within
the garden were obviously exploited to site
buildings that could command a view in all
directions. In this setting a gazebo could add
emphasis to a flight of steps or other major
structural element within the garden design.
A typical example might sit on the far side of a
broad terrace adjoining the house. Open
arches look to either side and out over the
lower garden levels, while the blank wall
closest to the house is host for climbing plants.
The roof, always desperately important,
should be simple and well constructed from
tiles that match the main building. All in all,
this would be an unfussy and totally worth
while feature.

A VARIETY OF STYLES

In a less architectural setting this little garden
house (Fig. 26) is set on a steep slope in
woodland. Here the construction is of brick
and timber, with viewing from all four sides.
The timbers are also arched and this leads the
eye up to the tiled roof, surmounted with a
ball – a humorous exclamation mark! Such a
building should be surrounded and smothered with climbing plants: *Clematis montana* or *Clematis tangutica* would be ideal in
light shade. Access by mown walks rather
than a formal paved path look just right and,
if a view can be obtained by cutting a clearing
through the trees this, too would be ideal.

Fig. 26 *What could be more delightful in a
woodland garden than this little gazebo. Set on
stilts with a pretty roof it would have an
unparalleled view over the slope.*

One of the best ways to site a summerhouse
or gazebo in the smaller garden, with no
views to the outside, is to set it in the angle
formed by two walls or boundaries. If such a
corner can be elevated, then so much the
better. Any upper level should be gained by
wide steps, into which can be incorporated a
generous landing for well-chosen pots. Once
at the top there should be an equally generous sitting area, which would have the benefit
of a diagonal view back across the lawn. If
there are garden walls they should be well
built and why not give them a superb coping
of tiles, which could match those used for the
gazebo roof. This question of linking
materials is well illustrated in the delightful
thatched gazebo shown in Fig. 27. Such a
composition has an undeniably rural feel and
this is heightened by the climber that forms a
canopy at the entrance. Inside there is a pool

Fig. 27 *For a really rural character thatch is hard to beat. Here the gazebo is softened by the fronds of* Clematis montana, *forming a frame to the pool of darkness within.*

of shade that works in direct contrast to the brighter light of the garden. Thatch is most definitely vernacular: use it with respect in the right setting and it will repay you handsomely. Abuse it by moving it away from a natural environment and it looks pretentious. The use of classical themes and borrowed materials has been with us since the Italian Renaissance and even earlier. In general such an approach needs to be handled carefully as such an obvious style stands out in sharp relief to its surroundings, particularly if these are of a different period. Another limitation has been the difficulty in obtaining such works and the inherent cost of these features.

Over recent years there has been a revival in classic themes, brought about partly by the need and desire to restore many fine buildings, and partly by a genuine interest in well proportioned and clearly defined ornamentation. In consequence a number of firms are engaged in manufacturing excellent repro-

ductions at a reasonable cost. Mostly this is carried out in reconstituted stone, although there are now several specialist joinery companies executing designs in timber.

On p. 83 is shown a small town garden that I constructed some years ago. It is essentially a formal design based on an asymmetrical pattern, a central canal dividing the space and providing unification. Instead of using old materials, modern equivalents were used, the paved areas and brick strips being constructed from concrete paving blocks. These are becoming increasingly popular, being cheap and easy to lay. The earlier types were produced in a range of dubious colours that included pink and green, but more recent additions are much closer to brick in appearance, and there are also an excellent range of clay paviors being made. They were first utilized to surface large areas used for parking, but are now employed with increasing success in gardens. As the edges of each module are chamfered, they can be butted close together, the resulting line being sufficiently strong to read as part of the overall composition.

The garden is entered at a point furthest from the pavilions, the boundaries being a combination of balustrade and concrete block walls. The latter are in fact an admirable walling material, particularly when they have a 'fair-face'. In this case they had a pleasing honey colour, this being dependent on the sand used for manufacture. When laid with narrow joints the end result is not unlike traditional Ashlar, but at a fraction of the cost. This colour is echoed in the gravel floor which should always be laid on 'hoggin' over a well compacted base of hardcore. It is a traditional approach but always ensure the loose surface is no more than 1 cm (0.5 in) thick, otherwise the end result resembles a treadmill. The pavilions guard the two bottom corners, looking back up the garden, the slender columns giving the buildings a degree of lightness that works in contrast to the strong line of the block wall that links them. Where roofs used to be built in tiles or slates, these are fibreglass. Such a material is ideally suited to this kind of work and can be moulded to a wide range of patterns. Here the roofs sweep upwards in a controlled manner, surmounted by a ball. Colour with fibreglass is critical, because if not made carefully it can end up looking cheap, which it is not. It can successfully match nearly all metals – lead, copper or simple ironwork. In this particular setting the roofs should have been lifted slightly higher, so that the complete line was visible. In such an architectural situation planting can be correspondingly positive. The Cordyline to one side and the handsome leaves of Rheum to the other are the perfect foil for the clean lines of stone. As well as the rear wall providing a link between the pavilions so, too, does the planting, this

A cold spring is not always conducive to sitting in the garden but what could be more attractive than this magnolia and thatched summerhouse?

being contained in a raised bed both to soften the wall and give young individuals an initial boost.

The buildings give this garden stability, partly due to the nature of the design and their size, the highest vertical element in the composition. To prevent the whole pattern appearing too severe, the water acts to tone down the surfaces, setting up reflections and providing movement. The stepping-stones are positioned precisely to 'float' on the surface, a slightly unnerving feature, but quite stable.

CONSTRUCTION

Although such pavilions look complicated, they can in fact be constructed relatively easily. As many similar buildings are available 'off the peg', it is worth looking at just how they are put together. They are usually delivered to the site packed carefully in individual sections. All the longer pieces of stonework are solidly reinforced with steel rod but, even so, columns can crack if dropped, so if you tackle the job yourself get at least three other people to help you. Accurate setting out and measuring is also vital. All the main weight is carried on the columns and you will need solid foundations of concrete at least 45 cm (18 in) deep under the corners, into which steel 'starter' rods for the columns can be set. Slightly shallower strip foundations are required under the balustrade runs, while the floor should have a base of well consolidated hardcore, subsequently 'blinded' with ash or sharp sand.

The Doric columns should be erected first and it is a great help to have adequate staging or, even better, a tower scaffold to hand. Special cement should be used which will match the stonework, and this too can be obtained from the manufacturer. Once the columns are in place, carefully fitted over the steel starter bars that have been cast into the foundations, it is wise to leave the job for a couple of days to allow the cement to harden off. Next the lintels are carefully lifted into position and steel dowels used to locate them accurately on the columns. Once these are in position the whole structure has permanent stability, and after another wait of two days the fibreglass roof can be fitted by drilling, plugging and finally screwing it home into the lintels. In my experience the floor should be laid next, and this should be very carefully set out, remembering that the balustrade, which comes last, has to fit exactly between the columns. To eliminate any chance of the slabs rocking, I would lay them on a continuous semi-dry mix of three parts sand to one part cement, or at the minimum five spots of mortar under each slab. One word of warning is that these slabs often tend to be softer than some of the 'patio' stones produced by other manufacturers. This makes them agreeably easy to cut with a power saw, but just as easy to break if you drop them!

As an extra degree of ornamentation a star can be laid as the centre slab, usually best in black or red and to help enliven what is a simple but slightly austere building. The last job is the balustrade and, if you have not laid one before, this can be a frustrating job. The base comes first, laid on the same special mortar mix over the previously prepared foundations. Make sure this is absolutely true, using a spirit level and straight edge.

The balusters follow and here it is useful to have an old cross-cut file to hand. This is because the stonework is cast by a hand process that leaves a slightly uneven surface, delightful as a finish but sometimes just a little awkward for construction. File off any irregularities in the top and base which will be invisible once the whole thing is put together. Dowelling is again used to fit the balusters to the base and the top, an operation that is best carried out simultaneously.

Some manufacturers do not drill the base and top and these should be reamed out accordingly with a power drill fitted with a masonry bit. As the building is tall and slender it is not advisable, in visual terms, to set it

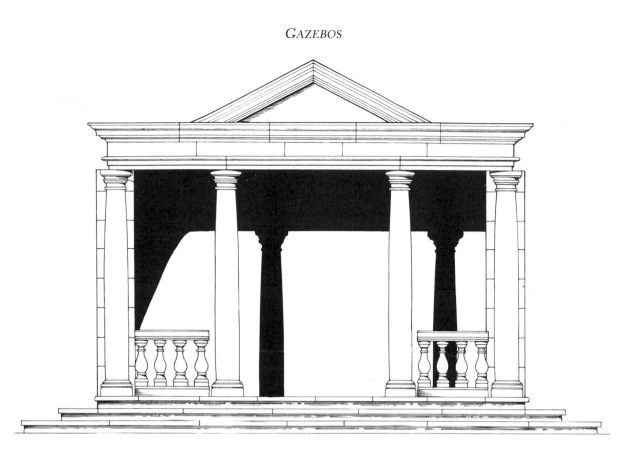

Fig. 28a   *A classic garden house sets a positive theme that is
strongly architectural. Such a design needs equally strong planting to
blend it into the wider garden.*

on a plinth. The rather more elaborate 'Etruscan Garden House', being essentially lower and longer (Fig. 28a), looks very good raised perhaps 45 cm (18 in) with three broad steps running up to it.

This is probably beyond the scope of most home garden builders, but it could be tackled by anyone with reasonable bricklaying experience, or a competent builder. In a garden of reasonable size, it would form a superb focal point and would be a telling statement in the larger landscape where it could be part of, or take in, a fine view. The basic components are much the same as for the little pavilions, with Doric columns and balustrade. Here, though, are added the classic components of a cornice and pediment. Internally the walls are of rendered breeze block which can be subsequently painted, perhaps with murals if you are ambitious. The outside is built from solid reconstituted stone blocks. These can look superb well laid, being very close in appearance to Ashlar. Keep the joints narrow

and use a suitable mortar mix. The floor looks particularly fine if built to a diagonal pattern and if the slabs are laid alternately red and white, to mimic a style popular 200 years ago. This is a big building by present day landscape standards, so use plenty of planting as a backdrop, with the accent on trees and evergreens.

A final example of this style could provide the basis of an elaborate trick in any town garden, particularly if the latter is surrounded by high walls. False doorways have long been a device for giving an impression of, if not greater space, at least a way through to a garden beyond. The doors can be faithfully painted or real, the addition of a deep architrave around the frame making them *very* real (Fig. 28b). Steps, as shown here, certainly add a little useful pretention, while the columns bear an elaborate roof, complete with balustrade. Against the wall, special half columns are snugly fitted, echoing the Doric style of the complete front set. Instead of a

balustrade in this position, I have seen a well detailed solid top that formed a raised bed. Lightweight soil was used and the area is big and deep enough to need only occasional watering. With or without the doors it makes a delightful, if slightly overblown, sitting area.

A garden of quite different conception is shown in Fig. 29. This is constructed on a sloping site, approximately 12 m (40 ft) square, using largely traditional materials. The whole design is set at an angle to the boundaries and the pool. The latter is set centrally, superbly constructed, and boasts a broad brick wall that lifts the water level to the height of a seat. The brickwork is in fact the dominant feature in this garden and it is interesting to note that this is always kept to a minimum width of 23 cm (9 in). Any less, as so often seen in garden walling, simply looks mean. The small lawn is semi-circular, repeating the shape of the pool, and having a cleverly constructed mowing edge of bricks laid flat that keeps a machine away from the wall that carries the ramped path.

FINDING A STYLE

The garden rises in a series of tiers away from the house, reaching a climax in the gazebo at the top of the garden. Unfortunately it is almost impossible to get well designed garden buildings of this type at a reasonable price. In consequence they have to be designed as 'one off' features, which in many cases puts them beyond the reach of the average gardener. In this particular situation I wanted something that was essentially simple. It had to fit into a contemporary design with considerable strength of purpose, and be practical at the same time. As it turns out it does all these things, but the basic

Old peg tiles and half timbering engender a sense of maturity to this modern gazebo, set in the corner of an equally contemporary garden.

91

Fig. 28b *This false door is framed by four columns that support a well planted bed. This is essentially an urban composition and would look out of place elsewhere.*

pattern is taken from a rural bus shelter a few miles from my home in Buckinghamshire. I suspect it was built between the wars with local labour and materials. In its original position, as here, it blended perfectly – were that so with bus shelters today! There is nothing complicated about its construction, using mellow brick and seasoned timber, and the latter being fashioned into simple arches that take the eye up to the roof in much the same way as the woodland example on p. 84. The roof itself is built from secondhand peg tiles – not always easy to find these days, but well worth the effort if you do. Its overall design keeps the building relatively low, important in this situation where a high roof, on rising ground would have provided far too much vertical emphasis. The bonnet tiles on the hips are particularly attractive, and this

type of attention to detail pays off in aesthetic terms.

The floor in all such pavilions or gazebos is another important detail. So often an excellent effort is spoilt by lack of thought. Where a building lacks a door, as in this case, there should be continuity between inside and out. Poorly laid concrete next to fine old slabs or brick simply will not do and looks particularly obvious. Here the small terrace is built in a combination, the brick filling in areas between the York stone flags. This is continued inside the building and more than justifies the relatively small additional cost involved.

Planting is again vital, both to tie the building into the garden and to soften its outline. Here it is handled well, the pot of white nicotiana, white azalea 'Persil' and lilacs helping to temper the stronger crimson

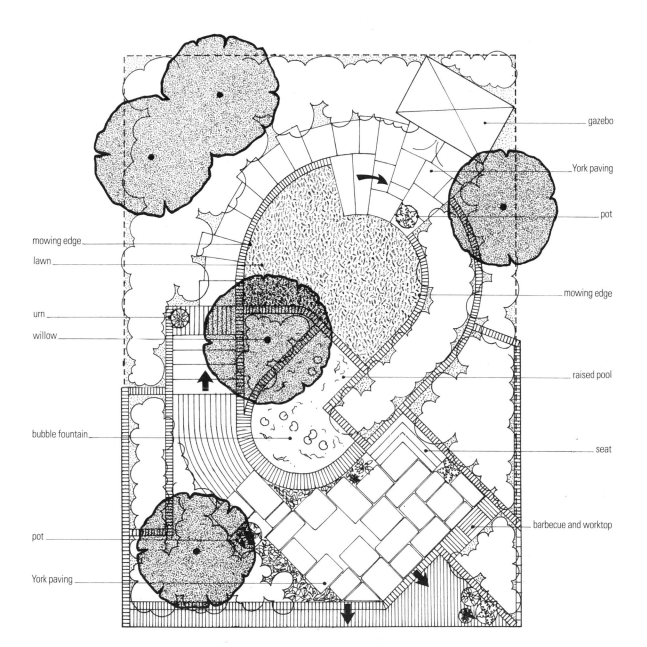

mowing edge

lawn

urn

willow

bubble fountain

pot

York paving

gazebo

York paving

pot

mowing edge

raised pool

seat

barbecue and worktop

Fig. 29 *The gazebo in this garden stands at the highest point with an attractive view back towards the house. Curves soften the design with the raised pool acting as a central pivot.*

rhododendrons. The fence behind is mercifully simple but would have looked better stained a darker brown to echo the woodwork of the gazebo.

This is a modern garden, using traditional materials and techniques. It is easy to run and restful on the eye, and admirably fits a con-

temporary life style.

A garden of slightly different proportions is shown in Fig. 30. Here the plot is longer than it is wide, approximately 11.5 m × 16.75 m (38 ft × 55 ft). The site is again sloping, with a gentle rise of about 1.25 m (4 ft) from the house. The brief in this case was to provide a

Thatch, although having a limited lifetime, is quite superb in the garden. This roof is supported by solid tree trunks, made all the more telling by delicate windows.

Opposite: This arbour has a slightly municipal feel, although the copper roof sets up fascinating dialogue with the coniferous backdrop and surrounding lawns.

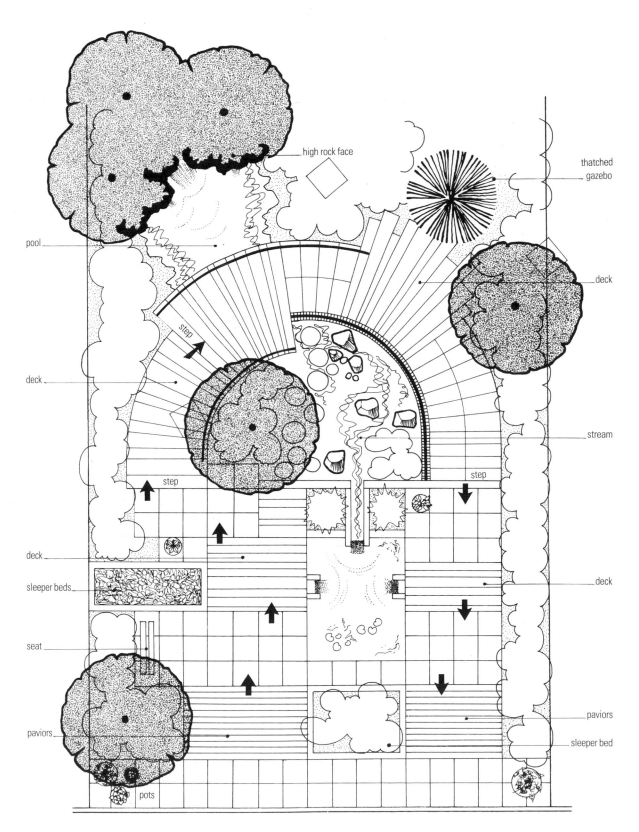

high rock face

thatched
gazebo

pool

deck

step

deck

stream

step

step

deck

deck

sleeper beds

seat

deck

paviors

sleeper bed

paviors

pots

Fig. 30 *The geometry of this design is tempered by superb planting,
water flowing from top to bottom of the slope. The gazebo is
thatched and flanked by a solid timber deck.*

garden that was simple to maintain, with water and rock as a dominant feature, and that could be viewed from all positions. It should also look as natural as possible. Moving away from the house, I provided a terrace of ample size using 0.5 m × 0.5 m (2 ft × 2 ft) Cotswold colour precast concrete paving slabs, teamed with a hard brown engineering brick. The latter, used alone, can look clinical, but its smooth surface and strong colour can form an attractive foil to other less architectural materials. It also has the advantage of being immune to frost, which can quickly ruin less durable brick paving. As the garden was to have a natural theme, timber plays a dominant role, being used first in the raised beds that give the main sitting area emphasis. These are constructed from railway sleepers, not laid one on top of another, but cut into sections and arranged vertically. The tops are set at different levels, producing an intentionally uneven line, 5 cm or 8 cm (2 in or 3 in) separating each sleeper. When planted, this slightly castellated effect is most attractive and sets up a positive rhythm. Semi-mature trees give height, and these help to frame the paths that lead up the slope and around the garden. Timber-decking forms a positive link with the solid sleepers used elsewhere in the garden and, if regularly swept, stays free from slime, ensuring a firm foothold. The decking and paths are all based off a central radius set in the bog garden and this, too, helps give the design its continuity.

THATCH

The main focal points are provided by the high rockface to one side, and the pretty thatched gazebo to the other. The former is a spectacular feature, over 2.5 m (8 ft) high from the top of the waterfall to the pool below. Rock, in this situation, has to look the part and a few large, well chosen pieces are far more effective than a miserable collection of small chunks. The 'currant bun' syndrome

is particularly apt in such surroundings! The pool empties through a stream under the deck, flows through the bog garden and finally drops into the rectangular tank that links visually into the crisper paving close to the house. This treatment is one of the prime rules of good garden design and states that an area close to the building should be predominantly architectural. Distance brings informality and this gradation of space provides visual depth to any composition.

A heavy wing of planting separates the rock face from the gazebo and the latter is unashamedly 'bosky'. It is thatched, with the eaves sweeping down on either side of the entrance. The top is prettily decorated, as all the best thatch should be, while the floor is a continuation of the decking that forms the pathway outside. Planting is particularly important here and should take the form of a fragrant climber. Roses are a possibility: the climber 'Étoile de Hollande', with its gorgeous double deep red flowers, would be hard to beat, and it's fragrant too. Summer jasmine is perhaps a little too delicate in line, so the best choice might be honeysuckle. Choose our own native *Lonicera periclymenum*, the woodbine of hedge and spinney. It is a vigorous plant which will scramble over a gazebo in double quick time. The flowers are large and very fragrant, being borne throughout summer until September, after which there is the bonus of red berries. If it becomes too rampant it can easily be cut back, being quick to regenerate. Such a canopy forms a soft frame around the entrance. Inside, in the cool shade, one is virtually invisible – contact with the outside world on a lazy summer afternoon is inadvisable in such conditions!

In all these gardens, the gazebo plays an important role, but one that is part of the composition rather than an overblown attention seeker. The lesson is simply one of considered good design, as all garden features are subservient to the overall pattern. One should never dominate at the expense of others.

Water has an inherent charm and when one can contemplate such a delightful view from a pretty summerhouse, the work involved in creating the composition is immediately worthwhile.

WATER

Although these last gardens have used water, it has been on the move. Still water, in large expanses, has an irresistible attraction that begs for a quiet place from which to view it. For those lucky enough to have a country garden and a lake, the opportunities are endless, but alas few of us are in that position. A little gem of a building, in which to dream a little, would take the form of a gazebo on stilts that would jut out over the shallows. Reached by steps, a timber deck blends with the woodwork of the building, while a thatched roof would again be perfectly complementary. If the deck is big enough, and visitors and children sensible, there is absolutely no need for a railing at the front. Picnics should be taken sitting on big cushions, which does away with the artificiality of chairs and brings one closer to the water, with definite aesthetic benefits. Sunbathing on a deck, with the gentle lap of water underneath is very close to heaven on earth, and does away with a nautical tendency towards queasiness. There is also enormous scope for planting, with the strong vertical line of rushes and reeds combining with the vast horizontal leaves of rheum, gunnera and rogersia.

There is sometimes the opportunity in a garden of reasonable size to at least hint at this technique, and if there is a natural stream you may just be able to create an artificial lake. If you do this, then the 'spoil' can be used to form gentle contours that can partly hide a well sited gazebo from the house. Such rising ground is the ideal host to lightly foliaged trees such as birch or, in milder climates, Eucalyptus. Imagine a stepping-stone path leading from the house to cross the stream by a simple bridge, terminating at a similarly paved sitting area in front of the gazebo.

The paving is laid informally with wide joints that allow the introduction of low aromatic thymes. In this situation, with naturally low ground and a relatively high water table, the lake can be formed simply by first stripping the topsoil, using a mechanical excavator. The subsoil is then scooped away on either side of the stream, with sheet metal temporarily lining the banks to keep the working area dry. The surrounding lawns and banks are then gently graded down to the proposed new water level, with the subsoil being used to create the contoured bank between the lake and the house.

The final job is to remove the sheet metal and allow the water to flow into the newly formed lake area. A simple sluice maintains a constant water level in even the driest conditions. Now the gazebo might have a superb view not only looking over the water but into the countryside. It is always a pity to skimp on space in this sort of situation, as such a building becomes the focal point of not just the garden but the family as well. For children it is a play house, for grown-ups a combination of somewhere that is both entertaining and a simple retreat. Facing west, it catches all the afternoon and evening sun, and once the planting around the lake margins has taken hold, it provides an ideal viewpoint for watching wildlife. The gazebo design is based on a pattern constructed around the turn of the century, being 'L' shaped with a delightful roof that sports a small conical tower, surmounted by a weathervane (Fig. 31). The roof flares out slightly over the eaves and this imparts a slightly oriental feel. In fine weather the French doors can be opened around two sides of the building, allowing one to sit in shade and at the same time take full advantage of the view.

A PATINA OF AGE

One problem in this little building, which was built of fine random local stone, was the fact that the latter, when first laid, looked very 'raw'. This is a common problem with all stonework and most particularly for the reconstituted types we considered earlier. Tra-

Fig. 31 *This grand gazebo verges on being a summerhouse with ample room for sitting and dining. With generous French doors the views are maximized and access onto the terrace made easy.*

ditionally the solution was to use cattle slurry, applied at various dilutions with a brush. The result was to encourage the growth of lichens and algae by providing an 'attractive' organic layer. It was effective but unapproachable, for obvious reasons, for quite some time! A far easier and less noxious solution uses the liquid manures that can be obtained from any good garden shop. Simply dilute to a strength of eight to one and slap it on: no smell, and not much mess. It turns the stone slightly darker, which happens with age anyway, and soon generates the required nutritional feeding ground for plant life that gives a building such as this a much needed look of maturity.

As well as these tiny plants, it was also important to think of the main structural planting that would give the building a sense of purpose and help it to blend into the overall garden setting. Trees are indispensable, but with a new stone building, constructed conventionally, one has to be conscious of the possible damage caused by an over-vigorous root system. Engineers, surveyors and some architects will tell you that a tree should never be planted closer to a building than the eventual height of the former. In other words, if a species grows to 15 m (50 ft), then that is the distance away it should be planted. As a general rule the spread of a root system matches that of the canopy – the furthest point spanned by the branches. Young trees obviously put on more growth and have a more vigorous root system than older, mature specimens. Placing a building close to a fully grown tree is less hazardous, as the root system has slowed right down.

More important for both young and old trees is the type of subsoil, as certain types dry out and crack more easily than others. The classic problem soil is termed a 'shrinkable clay' and this phrase is trotted out with monotonous regularity by building professionals, who sometimes have not even checked or taken a trial boring to ascertain the exact structure. Such a soil can indeed cause problems, and any building that is constructed off concrete foundations may be subject to movement. Lighter timber or metal structures that sit on the surface will be unaffected. If you are thinking of building a complicated gazebo it might be worth while getting in touch with a professional who will be able to advise you accordingly. There is also the question of planning permission if the building is over a certain size. This varies from area to area, so check with your local planning department.

TREES

As far as trees are concerned, whatever the soil steer clear of the rampant willow and poplar families. Not only do they reach enormoous proportions in a short period of time, but they consume very large volumes of water, which will naturally have an effect on the surrounding land. It is understandable to be fond of weeping willow but please remember how big it gets – it can dwarf all but the largest garden. It looks superb close to water, the strong vertical line of leaf and branch working in opposition to the horizontal sheet of a lake, but never, never plant it in a small front garden!

Suitable trees include the smaller species. Of these try any of the birch, e.g. *Betula jaquemontii* for its superb silvery white bark and *Betula nigra* for its tolerance of damp conditions. Most of the Malus or flowering crab apples, are fine and so too are the Sorbus. Of these try *Malus* 'Veitch's Scarlet', an outstanding form with white flowers and red fruit or Sorbus hupehensis, with unusual white berries and brilliant autumn foliage.

If you want a weeping tree, grow *Pyrus salicifolia* 'Pendula', the weeping silver-leaved pear. Silver it most certainly is, and sheer magic on a lawn in slightly misty weather when it shimmers with water droplets. A real favourite, and one that always retains its charm, is *Robinia pseudoacacia*

'Frisia', the golden-leaved Acacia. Hardly ever too large for even a modest garden, it looks particularly fine planted alongside the purple foliage of Cotinus or *Corylus maxima* 'Purpurea', the purple-leaved filbert.

Closer to home, bold foliage shrubs look particularly handsome against a small garden building, and one of my own choices would be the common fig, *Ficus carica*. Grow it in a sunny aspect and you will have fruit as well as those huge lobed leaves. Another choice might be that unusual bigeneric hybrid, *Fatshedera*, a cross between *Fatsia* and *Hedera*. It is tolerant of virtually any conditions, soil, shade and pollution, and it is a terrific plant in a dark town garden leaning against a white gazebo. It's evergreen too.

COUNTRY GARDENS

It is a fact that many country gardens are awkward shapes, and I recently worked on one where a lane bordered one side, a field the other, with the garden compressed by the two into a point at the far end. As with a town garden, the solution of 'space division' works admirably, but this time in a much looser manner. There may be an informal paved area close to the house and this can run gently into the lawns that surround two sides of the building. A few old fruit trees half way down the garden were kept for their spring blossom and strength of character, being supplemented by new varieties with greater fruiting potential. This small orchard divided the garden and was floored with rougher grass, naturalized with bulbs for spring colour and wild flowers for summer. A mown path winds its way between the trees and opens onto another lawn, this time much narrower, and focusing onto the charming little thatched gazebo shown in Fig. 32. To paint such a building would be quite wrong. It is treated instead with a clear preservative that simply highlights the beauty of the timber. The construction is straightforwardly rustic and

Fig. 32 *This 'beehive' gazebo has a pretty thatched roof and weatherboarded sides. It would form a focal point in any garden but needs siting with care and sensitivity.*

this is one setting where it is absolutely right. The shallow pointed arches provide a slight echo of the roof above.

In order to capitalize on the view, a section of old thorn hedge was removed and a short ha-ha constructed just inside the boundary. This is an old landscape device, much beloved by the great park builders of the eighteenth century. It involves digging a deep ditch that will prevent the invasion of livestock, but at the same time preserve the view. The bank is sometimes faced with stone and occasionally has a fence at the bottom. Although expensive to construct long runs, it can be cost-effective in the design shown here. A few hours of machine work, but quite possible by hand. Many field hedges also carry ditches that may be dry in summer but quite different in the wet. Do check this, and check with the farmer too, otherwise you may become the owner of a mini moat, a hazard to livestock and public relations alike. A final bonus here is the fine old oak tree that leans over the gazebo. Such a tree goes a long way to

providing stability for the overall composition, and it gives this building both a frame and a backdrop against which it can work. The worst thing for any gazebo, and particularly one in a rural setting, is to be dumped in isolation. The effect is totally flat and far too obvious. Always give it a background and always give it a purpose.

Finally before moving up to date to a contemporary garden situation, let us look at two traditional garden settings that both use charming brick-built gazebos. The first is in fact a pair, built not long after the turn of this century by Lawrence Johnston at Hidcote Manor in Gloucestershire. This fine garden, now run by the National Trust is notable for two things in particular: the subdivision of space to form separate garden rooms, each of which follows a particular horticultural theme, and the fact that the soil is very chalky. At the end of a grass walk, flanked by broad beds, a generous flight of steps climbs to a higher level. To emphasize this drama stand two fine pavilions, with superb roofs surmounted by stone finials. Beyond these the tension is increased by pleached hornbeams, clipped into a square that compress the line of the grass walk back to the width of the steps. This is garden planning at its expansive best and shows an interesting contrast to a true rural scene in a controlled manner that very much tempers plant material to the designer's will.

The second example is much older, dating from around the middle of the seventeenth century. It too is brick, and fits comfortably into the angle of heavily buttressed walls (Fig. 33). Ionic columns provide decoration at the corners and the first floor is elevated to a level that can look out across a timeless English countryside. The roof is peg-tiled, and the top surmounted by a simple lead ball. The result is undeniably beautiful.

But a lot of these buildings, by their scale,

really do exclude themselves from the modern domestic garden scene. Neither do they 'scale down' as so many manufacturers of garden buildings would have us believe. To reduce them simply ruins the proportions, and more often than not they end up looking pretentious.

OFF THE PEG

A typical 'off the peg' gazebo can form a very attractive focal point in a suburban garden and looks particularly good, for example, by the free flowing lines of a swimming pool. As with virtually all the buildings we have considered, it should nestle against a backdrop of mature planting that has been planned to provide colour and interest

Hidcote Manor is full of superb images, this gazebo being but one. The step and railings lead one gently through the change in level while the hedges frame the view.

103

Fig. 33 *There is little to beat the permanence and visual stability of brick. When this is teamed with fine old pan tiles the result is garden poetry.*

throughout the year. Swimming pools are often difficult features to integrate into a garden, their very size tending to dominate everything else. The cleanliness of the water, although setting up dramatic reflections, has a clinical overtone and this is often compounded by a crisp stone coping, surrounded by unrelenting precast concrete paving. In this garden I designed the pool into a slight slope, the inherent shape echoing the contours and providing a comfortable link with the landscape. Instead of a slabbed sitting area, I used brick paving, and this smaller module follows the shape of the pool, setting up a pleasant rhythm that is followed by the retaining wall at a higher level. In the little octagonal gazebo three of the arches have

been left open, the others being filled with diamond trelliswork. This acts in a number of ways and, looking through the arches from outside, you obtain a glimpse of foliage beyond that helps to 'lighten' the whole structure. And just as important to my mind is the reverse view, from inside to out. Here one is looking at the interplay of light and shadow, the archways creating a frame for differently angled garden views. This makes the siting of the gazebo all the more critical, for what may look fine as a view from the house may set up something quite different when gazing from the other direction. This is also a chance to see planting, and climbing plants in particular, in a completely different light. When sitting inside a gazebo one is looking at the frame of the building and the plants in silhouette, something we rarely consider from elsewhere in the garden.

LIGHTING

Apart from natural lighting, there is of course the whole question of artificial light during the evening and night. Many a garden is completely ruined by the halographic displays so beloved by some manufacturers, but the placing of well positioned subtle lights can do much to produce an entirely different dimension.

Lighting really falls into two categories: decorative and functional. The latter has obvious advantages for gazebos as well as for pergolas, arches and arbours. It can direct feet and eyes along a path and warn of any particular hazards on the way. A single light, or a number of low wattage bulbs can effectively illuminate a sitting area, but remember that in such a situation it is the illumination and *not* the fitting that is important. The awful pretension of street lights in gardens should be avoided at all costs. Far better to conceal a light in a tree or within a border.

While light some distance off the ground shines directly down, in much the same way as sunlight, ground level illumination is altogether different. Here we are seeing the underside of leaves and foliage which has a substance and texture all its own. The colour of light bulbs is also important – blue and white tend to be best, but red and orange turn foliage the most revolting hue. Green tends simply to wash things out. For ease of operation, and also practicality, a centralized switchboard in the main living room or suitable vantage point is a great help. Remember, too, that as a garden develops and trees grow, the effect of lights will change. Many modern systems utilize ground spikes or clamps which allows them to be adjusted quickly and easily. This is essentially a two person job, done at night, with one in the

house directing and the other moving the fitting. Needless to say, good systems are fully waterproofed and most work off a transformer that reduces the voltage to a minimal level in case of accident. Never try to bodge anything electrical in the garden, and always use fully waterproofed sockets and connections. If in any doubt, call in the serves of a qualified electrician; his charges will be well worth it.

When a gazebo or other similar feature is not in use, it can look marvellous lit from within. A pavilion with trellis sides smothered in climbing roses and clematis becomes a charming garden beacon, set in a pool of darkness. The method of light can either be by a conventional pendant, hung from the ceiling or, more dramatically, a swimming pool light set in the floor. The latter can look absolutely superb, particularly as the beam is usually soft and diffused. The temptation to 'dress' a gazebo at Christmas is almost irresistible and quite allowable in aesthetic terms!

The opposite of this, and a device I have only seen once, is a genuine lighthouse effect. This little garden house had a steeply conical roof, at the top of which stood a tiny dovecot. The doves had been long ousted and a light shone from the entrance holes. The effect was unexpected and not altogether unpleasant. Dovecotes were not at all uncommon on top of garden buildings. The fact of the matter is that they formed an important part of a diet several hundred years ago. To my mind their visual pleasure is far outweighed by the unending deposits of guano and the noise, which although charming in small quantities, becomes paranoic after any length of time. Doves also inter-breed freely with pigeons and over the years the snow-white variety quickly become piebald. I am still firmly convinced that they are of far more value on the table than in the garden.

Another little gazebo similar to that by the swimming pool is shown on p. 106. It is slightly lighter in appearance and this is largely due to the delicate glazing bars used in the

Opposite: *Such a pretty building deserves a special place in any garden – and not one that is immediately obvious. Surprise is an essential part of garden design.*

The view from this modern gazebo looks out over a timber deck, water, lawn and an envelope of controlled planting. See how the species are used in drifts to provide continuity.

windows, and the turned roof that doubles both as a gutter and gives the structure a slightly oriental feel. The building is circular in shape and the vertical boarding, together with the windows, increases the visual height.

Such a style is akin to some of the excellent reproduction conservatories available at the moment. More often than not these are natural extensions from a period house, but they can quite easily be modified by the manufacturer to become free standing units.

They look their best in white woodwork, and a great deal of the beauty is attributable to the attention paid to detail and the delicacy of their glazing. To be utterly romantic they need to be surrounded by pastel shades of flower, pear blossom at the highest level, dropping down to the massive heads of *Crambe cordifolia* or *Aruncus sylvester* (goat's beard). *Gypsophila* forms a perfect carpet at the lowest level of all. All this placed in an orchard setting with wild flowers would be quite irresistible.

Such a building is a far cry from the mass-produced summerhouse offered in so many catalogues and garden centres. To my mind these can never really qualify for the gazebo name-tag, and most look desperately suburban. Good siting and planting can help, but in the final analysis poor mass production is the antithesis of good garden ornamentation, of which the pavilion is part.

THE WAY FORWARD

Having looked at the spectrum of garden buildings and seen how these can be integrated into the contemporary setting, what direction can we expect such features to take in the future? Part of the answer is in integration. The garden room, summerhouse and gazebo coming together to form a functional space that can serve the whole family as well as a view. As a final example I show the view from just such a feature on p. 107. This is a small garden, measuring barely 15.25 m × 15.25 m (50 ft × 50 ft), in which the major theme is water. All the materials are natural, and the rear of the house opens onto a broad timber deck that is suspended over a large pool. The deck gives way to random placed stepping-stones that cross the lawn and work their way up the shallow stream. Broad timber steps mount the slope, being supported by solid timber uprights that give the composition a slightly Japanese feel. The open risers cast dark shadows and the fact that the stream issues from beneath them adds to the feeling of mystery. The steps are 'staggered' from side to side and this, in conjunction with the use of sculptural planting, gives the design great movement before reaching the main deck that adjoins the garden room. This too is floored in timber but, instead of having all the boards the same width, they vary providing inherent interest.

The deck is flanked by a raised pool, which accepts a cascade from a higher level of the garden, and on the opposite side of a built-in seat and barbecue, forming the perfect sitting and dining area. The building is low, long and unashamedly modern, the timber fascia board echoing the deck below. The walls are built from fair faced concrete blocks in a sandstone colour, a Chinese gooseberry, *Actinidia chinensis*, softening the strong horizontal line. Large glass sliding doors fit from floor to ceiling and these give a perfect view back over the deck and pool, towards the house. Such a simple, but severe building needs softening and this it gets from the superb backdrop of mixed planting that includes mature acer and rhododendron.

The building in this composition works in direct contrast to the extreme informality of the rest of the garden, which flows in and between the central line of the stream. The planting is well thought out and will need little maintenance with the high proportion of ground covering plants. The lawn is slightly problematical and would be best cut with a combination of lightweight rotary mower and strimmer, the latter being ideal near the water's edge and around the stepping-stones.

This is indeed a contemporary garden, but using conventional components. I am at present working on a scheme that will use a combination of plants, paving and fibre optics. The latter are not only being used to simulate 'light plants' but we are hoping to frame them into a glowing gazebo or arbour. The back and sides of the building will be designed with a mass of fibres, the ends of which will glow with delicate light. The doorway will be left open and one will be able to enter beneath a thatch of light. Such schemes are only for the very rich and would, to many gardeners, be the complete antithesis of all they hold dear. However, from a personal point of view I can see a tantalizing way forward, a combination that combines technology and living plant material. This is not taming nature, rather adding to it in a way that will open new horizons to all gardeners. If we look at garden buildings in this way there is a history of development stretching away to a point which we can no longer see.

5

Follies

There must be very few people in the country who are trustees of a folly. I am lucky enough to be one of them, having responsibility for the so-called Buckingham Gaol. Built by Lord Cobham, the Master of Stowe, it takes the form of a miniature castle with battlements, towers and all the outward signs of fortification. Its purpose, when erected in 1748, was to entice the county assizes back to Buckingham, the original county town, removed by the supposedly wicked Tories some years before. Cobham was a devout Whig, but all his efforts were in vain; the court stayed in Aylesbury and the Gaol was a dismal failure. One of the prisoners was even able to walk out through lack of security! Since then it has been variously an electricity substation, restaurant, antique shop and council office. It is now being painstakingly restored by a charitable company to its former glory, a white elephant of generous but lovable proportions.

FLIGHTS OF FANCY

This perhaps sums up the whole philosophy behind these extraordinary buildings which are outrageous flights of fancy. It is not possible to define accurately the very best follies, their charisma and appalling ostentation places them in the realm of mute admiration. If one has to analyse, then that analysis would state they are large and useless objects, set in a landscape to catch the eye. By this, the builder or owner has made a statement so outlandish as to elicit wonder, despair, or simple mirth from the onlooker. At the time they were built such emotions could be expressed directly to the eccentric in question, usually much to the gratification of the latter. They were, if you like, enormous autographs and, like handwriting, no two were, or ever are, alike. It also comes back to the refreshing theme of humour which we have encouraged in other parts of this book. Gardening snobs hate humour for the simple reason that they are afraid of seeming foolish. Not so the glorious folly fanatics. They were overblown, irreverent and full of fun, fun on the grandest scale of all, and fun of a kind that although less obvious in today's garden, is still in fact alive and possible,

So where did it all start, this desire for quirky but expensive humour? This is really lost in the depths of history and while the great age of the folly extended for about a hundred years, from 1725 to 1825, genuine examples can be traced back much further.

Like many types of garden and garden ornament follies are the culmination of a particular art form that in itself reflects if not decadence, at least cultural maturity. Examples are not readily discernable in the very earliest civilizations, but by the time the Roman empire flourished, there is definite historical evidence, some of which can still be seen today. Perhaps the best of these is a Hadrian's villa at Tivoli where a cave, hollowed out at vast expense and labour was turned into a Nymphaeum, the Greek and Roman equivalent of a grotto. This was sited at one end of a grand canal, lined by statues, and the grotto itself was a dining room of extreme ostentation. It was constructed partly underground and had a system of ingenious water features that spouted and dripped while feasting was in progress. Such a scene is difficult to comprehend in a temperate, damp and often cold climate, but in the warmth of the Mediterranean it must have been a welcome relief from the often overpowering sun.

To both the Romans, and more particularly the Greeks, water had strongly sacred overtones, with natural caves seen as the home of gods, and inevitably artificial grottos

109

followed suit, having religious significance and acting as a backdrop for statuary and ornamentation of all kinds.

Throughout the dark ages gardens were of minor importance, with men's minds turned to more hostile pursuits, but in the flowering of the Italian Renaissance the grotto, that most historic of all follies, again reared its head. Water in all its guises still retained its mythical roots and was used in all those exuberant shutes, falls, rills and fountains of such masterpieces as the Villa d'Este and the Villa Aldobrandini. The grotto still mimicked the earlier Nymphaeum with its dank interior and moisture-tolerant planting, setting a theme that was to be repeated with so much enthusiasm 300 years later in the more sombre light of England.

The French Renaissance, which culminated in the awe-inspiring but rigid splendour of Versailles, had little time or room for the miniature folly, but it could equally be argued that such a vast composition was in itself a folly. There were certainly some almost

If gnomes are your particular love then this chap is perfect. Never forget that humour is an inseparable facet of good garden architecture.

Opposite: *Follies conjure up images of eccentricity and mystery, epitomized by this gothic garden house framed on all sides by walls of foliage.*

110

unbelievable manipulations of land and water, the great canal being big enough to contain a large contemporary sailing ship. The philosophy of a ship with nowhere to sail is megalomania of the highest order and in itself sets the garden owner, in this case Louis XIV, apart from ordinary mortals. The grotto at Versailles was a victim of increasing expansionism and had to be demolished to make way for palace improvements. From all accounts it was a splendid affair with a roof studded with semi precious stones and mirrors.

After Versailles there was an understandable sigh of relief and the basic geometric garden frame, although still providing an underlying theme, was subject to wild and bizarre additions. On the continent different styles from all over the world added features that might genuinely be called follies, from the enormity of a 10 m (33 ft) statue of Hercules atop a pyramid in a garden at Wilhelmshohe, to a hill full of windmills at Potsdam.

All this was happening in the early part of the eighteenth century and at a similar time, in England, there were signs that the lethargy which the British have always displayed in landscape design, was being replaced by a genuinely radical and thoroughly indigenous school of thought.

We have already looked at the great landscape parks of Kent and Brown which were of so large a scale that the only real chance of ornamentation lay in the construction of not just vast mansions, but buildings set in the landscape as ornaments in their own right. At first these looked for inspiration back to the golden classical empires of Greece and Rome, with a wealth of temples and water features that could be linked directly to earlier great Italian gardens. It did not take long, however, for the English to really get to grips with this rather dull, but well proportioned form of decoration. Very soon, with wild enthusiasm born of impatience, they went completely potty. The rule book went out of the window and thankfully fun came back in.

ARCHITECTURAL ABERRATION

The interesting thing is that many respected and capable architects, with flourishing city practices, sneaked off to the country to dabble in flights of fancy at their delighted client's expense. This could be nothing but healthy; while the mainstream of architecture continued on its sober way, the landscape became a test bed for every conceivable style and whim.

If the landscape folly could be genuinely gross and in many instances employ good quality materials, the garden folly was usually on a smaller scale, utilizing cheaper construction. As a consequence, if the owner voiced dislike the object could be removed without excessive financial hardship. For the amateur folly builder there were a myriad pattern books that showed in more or less detail how to build a pyramid, lighthouse, crenellated pig-sty or hermit's hovel. No allegiance to national style was necessary, Greek, Egyptian, Scottish, Oriental or overblown romantic notions of rural England were all acceptable, along with anything else that took the fancy.

An acceptable definition of folly deems that it should be useless, and if it is a ruin then indeed there can be very little purpose served by such a structure. Many of what I classify as follies are slightly different, being built to look like one thing, when in fact they are another. This naturally confirms their uselessness for the former, but as far as the latter is concerned they may have had, and continue to have, a most worthwhile existence. The advantage of this type of folly is that its very nature ensures its preservation for the future; in other words it contributes in more than just visual terms. Of course history is only part of the story, and follies live on in today's landscape. I had enormous fun with an eccentric client who collected totem poles. These we set in a woodland, producing unexpected and often sinister focal points.

ANIMALS

The British have always been sentimental over animals, sometimes to the point of insanity. It is not surprising therefore that they constructed, and still do, monuments to their passing. A fine obelisk for an aristocratic pig stands near Plymouth, a mausoleum to of all things a racing pigeon and numerous highly ornamental tombs for dogs and horses. One of the most beautiful follies commemorates a horse. This can be found at Farley Down where a false spire rises in high drama against a Hampshire sky. The surrounding downland landscape and elevated position make it quite breathtaking. The story goes that the horse saved its owner by surviving a jump into a chalk pit. Such a monument, in such a setting, is certainly appropriate for a beast that spent its life galloping over it!

But if owners remember their animals in death, they can go to even greater extremes when they are alive. Birds seem particularly well endowed, and the second Duke of Dorset built a substantial gothic cottage for his. The Duke, like many of the best folly builders, was reputedly touched with madness, and a dubious poet to boot. On an even higher plane there is, at Wooton House in Surrey, a temple for tortoises. Today most people would consider this to be a total 'wind up' but this fine and expensive building was put up in about 1835, possibly by Francis Edwards, a well known architect of the period. It housed terrapins in a pool, which could be viewed while having tea, and in its heyday the garden was also host to a vulture and kangaroos.

Temples in honour of, or as enclosures for, animals are not uncommon, but the best of the lot must be the Grecian temple for pigs at Fyling Hall in North Yorkshire. The latter is rather better known today for its early warning radar domes that are appropriate follies of a totally different kind. The temple was built under the eccentric directions of a certain Mr. Barry, the owner of the Hall. He gathered architectural ideas from all over the world and wove them into a splendid sty. A grand elevated front sports six Ionic columns surmounted by a fine pediment; the top of which must be 12 m (40 ft) above the ground. The pigs were probably pretty sanguine about the whole thing.

Living in Buckingham, a small country town in the north of the county of the same name, we are exceptionally lucky. Stowe Park lies just three miles away and within its boundaries are contained more follies, garden buildings, temples and the like than anywhere else in the world. Many of these are simply ornamental, being the culmination or starting point for a particular view or vista. Two of my favourites, which I pass every day are rather more than that.

The Corinthian arch is a splendid monument, which is viewed from the south front of the main house. It stands on the crest of a hill which rises gently in a classic pastoral landscape from the lake at its foot. It marks the end of a vista from the house, but the start of an avenue nearly two miles long that runs in a direct line into the town of Buckingham. It is reputedly only the beginning of a road that was to lead to London and Buckingham Palace; indeed a folly.

But the arch is more than what it appears, and if you approach it on foot the scale soon becomes obvious. It is huge and within each side is located a cottage of limited but adequate proportions. Steps lead to the top of the arch and the view from here is not only stupendous but one that can only have been experienced infrequently, particularly by the owners of Stowe itself.

My other favourite is Stowe Castle, now outside the grounds and designed by Gibbs in 1740. From three sides it is a gaunt, battlemented stone castle of small but nevertheless imposing proportions. On a cold winter's day it rises above the ploughed fields with an undeniably sinister outline. On the fourth, open, side approached by a minor road, there is no building, just a central gravel courtyard. Here the architecture is particularly delicate, with delightful ogee windows that

Opposite: *All the best follies are useless and here a spiral staircase goes precisely nowhere up this cleverly contrived tower. The painted interior is particularly curious.*

Heathers form a restless setting for this pseudo-crumbling ruin. A more authentic approach would have used sombre evergreens and dripping ferns.

produce a feeling of intimacy and an agreeable welcome. Such a building is the best kind of landscape humour which has stood the test of time to become a pleasantly idiosyncratic home.

The trouble with follies is that they are catching – the more you see, the more you want to see. Let us just look at a few more of my favourites; it may well whet your appetite to become a folly seeker in your own right.

MAD JACK FULLER

In many instances the name alone has enormous attraction and mystery, and Mad Jack Fuller was perhaps the best of them. He acquired wealth from an early age and with genuine gusto spent his life getting rid of it. Born in 1757, and dying at the considerable age of 77, his life spanned the golden age of follies and he certainly made the most of it. He was a total demagogue, swore repeatedly at the Speaker of the House of Commons, refused a peerage and was fiercely parochial to his home county of Sussex. He lived at Brightling Park and built many eccentric buildings, the best known of which is Mad Jack's Sugar Loaf. Built as a wager to imitate a local church spire, which he swore could be seen from his house, it was typical of his impulsive nature. It still stands in the park as an unlikely, and like many of its counterparts, a slightly frightening prospect. This is perhaps one of the major emotions to do with follies. Because they have no real purpose, and because of their size and complete antithesis to their surroundings, they still have the ring of madness that was the basis of their creation. There is the genuine smell of fear in many of them that elicits relief in departure.

As a last historical glimpse, how about an underwater ballroom, a genuine dance floor below a lake? This would seem unlikely even in today's advanced technology, but one was built and still survives. It was constructed as part of a fantastic scheme by Whitaker Wright, a multi-millionaire even at the turn of this century. His house stood at Witley Park near Godalming, and the feature to which I refer was only one of a number of follies. To reach the ballroom you can take two routes: one a straightforward underwater tunnel about 30 m (100 ft) long, which is remarkable enough in its own right, but the really unbelievable way in is tortuous and atmospheric in the extreme. You enter by an extraordinary door set in a tree in a wood some distance away. A spiralling ramp leads down to various ever darker chambers, at the bottom of which, in total darkness, lies a subterranean canal. This can be navigated in a small boat, bringing you eventually to a lake, on the middle of which is a small island. Once ashore you go down more steps until at last you are in a real domed ballroom, completely under water and completely dry. The fact that it is still dry, nearly 90 years after it was built, is a credit to both Wright and the engineers that put it all together. The technology that was born from the Industrial Revolution, which on the whole spawned the wealth to create these fantasies, was advanced indeed.

MODERN TRENDS

But it was wealth that made all this happen, and even the most modest folly would be horrendously expensive by today's standards. So how can this quirky eccentricity live on, and indeed is it still with us? The fact that the Englishman considers his garden to be his castle sums up the whole philosophy: it is simply coincidental that the area under his direct control has become even smaller. Taken to extremes the same person that built Sugar Loafs or Terrapin Temples, jumps into his car and descends upon his local garden centre. Rustic summerhouses, tortuous fibre glass pools and halographic rotating lighting kits have the ring of soft headedness that goes back through generations of garden makers. On today's domestic scene the garden gnome can trace his history back through a distinguished lineage: he is a thoroughbred over and over, and any of those gardening snobs who turn up their noses know nothing at all. If somebody wants a little fellow leaning on a rake in front of their finest hosta, then good luck – the only difference between them and Mad Jack Fuller, is cash.

But gnomes apart it really is still possible to create a garden centred around a folly of some magnitude and it needed not necessarily cost the earth.

Some time ago I was commissioned to do just this, in a small garden barely 15.25 m (50 ft) square. Because of its limited size this had to be a total composition, the folly if you like had to be the garden. The brief, following in the best folly tradition was right over the top. A traditional overshot water mill that had to look at least 200 years old, a head race, tail race, large pools and a bridge. When you view the finished result it all looks relatively straightforward but the planning along the way had to be impeccable. The initial problem was in many ways the most drastic. The site was virtually flat and to create an elevated mill and a water supply that at least looks as though it is coming from higher ground behind, would not be easy. The first task was of course to create the design, which had to work in visual as well as practical terms. Moving away from the house there needed to be a flat paved area of ample size to provide room for all the normal garden functions of sitting, eating and entertaining. This was to be paved in fine old rectangular York stone, which although initially expensive, will last a lifetime and moreover look the part.

When choosing stone of this nature steer clear of the thin 'riven' type that is advertised regularly in Sunday papers and the garden press. More often than not it is split into thicknesses of less than 2.5 cm (1 in) and this weakens it considerably, making it particularly prone to frost attack. Good second hand York can be between 8–10 cm (3–4 in) thick. It is very heavy and not easy to lay, but it is well worth the effort. Avoid also the broken or crazy-paving. Admittedly this is cheaper, but it is also an inherently 'fussy' material that always tends to clash with the cleaner, more architectural lines, of a building. If you are going to use this type of surface then relegate it to the further, less formal parts of a garden, where it can blend more easily into a natural setting.

The whole centre section of the garden is given over to water, to form the mill pond, fed from the tail race. An old timber bridge, made from simple sawn planks, spans the pool, each timber being cut individually to match the radius that turns the bridge through an angle to reach the steps. Once there, another paved area opens up to form a raised terrace. To one side of this stands the mill, to the other an old brick-built arbour, the beams and timbers acting as hosts for scrambling *Clematis montana*. The real link between upper and lower parts of the garden, apart from the millstream, is the serpentine brick wall that sweeps in a flowing 'S' shape from the steps right around the lower pool and finishes near the front of the garden.

BUILDING A MILL

So much for the design. What about the constructional problems? The first task was to achieve the necessary changes of level and to create sufficient height to allow water to flow over the mill wheel. Although the site was not on a hill, there was a slight gradient up from the house, and to create greater drama a 'cut and fill' technique was used. The ground nearest the house was levelled, which necessitated cutting into the slope. This soil, together with the spoil from the pool, was heaped up at the back of the garden to form the basis of a well planted bank that would simulate a woodland with an associated stream. The timbers for the mill had been cut out of a copse some months before. The wood was elm, and a victim of Dutch Elm disease. Elm is in fact ideal for this kind of work,

A decorative watermill is eccentricity of the best
kind and here everything works, including the
underlying garden design. The planting is quite
superb and the attention to detail impeccable.

Opposite: In this close up view the waterwheel,
mill race and bridge are all clearly visible. It is
hard to believe that the building is genuinely
modern although all the materials are antique.

because it is a hard wood, very slow to rot and
almost completely water resistant. It is traditionally used for lining canal banks, spend-
ing its life under water. For antique work of
this nature it is also ideal, as the timber often
twists after a few years in the open, adding to
the patina of age.

The mill was to be of a half timber construction and it was essential that the timbers
were weathered down. This was achieved by
stripping the bark and then burning the wood
surface with a blow lamp. This exposes the
weaker sections of grain which are then
rubbed away lengthways using a wire brush.
The process is repeated and then painted
with a matt oil-based paint. Once this is
soaked in, the timbers are again 'distressed'
by wire brushing and judicious blow lamp
treatment. All this work is carried out before
the lengths are fitted together, constructional
work helping to add to the overall ageing. The
timbers that form the main support of the
building are built off-minimal foundations as
any slight ground movement adds to the

character! Construction is traditional, utilizing mortice and tenon joints that are fixed
with wooden dowels, the latter being left
proud of the surface for 'effect'. Don't worry
if you feel this is a little ostentatious; all the
best follies suffer from a liberal helping of
this! The floor is simply beaten earth, the roof
felted, battened and fitted with good old peg
tiles. Don't skimp on the latter, they may be
expensive and hard to get but the newer
substitutes are quite unacceptable.

Roofs are always eye-catchers, so get them
right. The mill wheel was quite a job, also
made from elm and liberally coated with hot
pitch to make it completely waterproof. It
was mounted in a pit, which was in fact a
butyl rubber-lined sump which would house
a submersible pump. A steel spindle and
roller bearing carried the wheel from the
arbour support on one side to the mill wall on
the other. It was so well balanced that before
the sump was filled it could be turned with
one finger. A water shute was fitted from the
back brick wall of the arbour to a support on

the side of the mill, water being pumped from the sump, via a pipe, to the rear of the shute and then down over the wheel. In fact a trickle would turn the latter and the water in the sump had to be raised to a level where it covered the bottom 23 cm (9 in) of the wheel, thus acting as a brake.

On the other side of the 'old' ladder that led up to the loading platform, the tail race issued through a beautifully built brick culvert. This too was cleverly constructed to look as if the water was flowing down from the wheel, but the latter is a closed system, just feeding itself. The tail race is fed by a pipe from the mill pond, where another submersible pump recirculates a separate water system.

The pond is constructed from a large butyl sheet, laid on a bed of soft sand. The sand acts as a cushion, preventing the considerable water pressure bearing down on to any sharp projections. At the front of the garden, close to the main terrace, the liner is carried under the damp 'bog' garden which provides the ideal environment for a wide range of moisture loving plants, finally tucked under the York stone at a slightly higher level.

The planting of this garden is superb, with the acid soil acting as a perfect host for a wide range of rhododendron and azalea. Many of the plants were already semi-mature which also allowed the framework to be built up more quickly. The bog plants are particularly attractive, using many indigenous species that include water forget-me-nots, meadow sweet and the ever useful marsh marigold, *Caltha palustris*.

A final glance at the mill will show that it is well endowed with all the authentic bolts, handles and rusty nails that should grace any folly of this type, even down to the horseshoe on the door. If you become a folly builder the prime rule which, if you are not careful becomes an obsession, is to hoard any item of old and seemingly useless equipment. This does nothing to improve matrimonial relations, but it is an invaluable store when you need 'that one thing' to put the icing on the cake.

This is a domestic folly of some ingenuity and considerable scale, but none of it beyond the scope of a competent amateur builder. The most important point about the construction as a whole is the fact that the mill has never had to do anything, although it could drive a small generator, trip hammer or – heaven forbid – a string of fairy lights.

ARE THEY ON SALE?

Having said all this, is there anything possible on a smaller scale, or even something that can be bought 'off the peg'? In Milton Keynes, the new city in Buckinghamshire, there are situated the famous concrete cows (Fig. 34). These are visual relations of our friendly gnomes and are a simple joke. If it was not for their notoriety they would pass very well for the real thing, at a distance; it is only when you get relatively close, particularly on a cold, misty winter's morning, that the deception becomes apparent. They were originally set in concrete, but one or more enterprising persons rearranged them recently into a suggestive pose that indicated the possibility that more calves might be on the way. Living sculpture at its best!

This introduces the question as to whether statuary can fall into the folly category. I would suggest it can, but there has to be something that raises it above the run-of-the-mill garden ornament. Size is one obvious candidate, gnome world at one end and Jack and the Beanstalk at the other. A friend of mine once managed to lay his hands on the giant of this story, that was previously the property of a film company. He had it sited in his orchard and he took great delight in frightening the life out of visitors on a quiet stroll through the old fruit trees.

Another devastatingly effective but smaller device lies just outside a hamlet known as The Lee in central Buckinghamshire. In a twisting country lane with high hedges on either side one is suddenly confronted by a

Fig. 34 *The famous Milton Keynes Cows are more than just an artistic joke, they are part of a tradition that dates back to the grand folly builders of the eighteenth and nineteenth centuries. As long as gardeners retain a sense of humour there is always scope for original thought.*

bizarre and vividly painted bust, rearing over one side of the road. It is in fact a ship's figure head, lovingly restored but very real. It is genuinely surprising and not guaranteed to keep the motorist's mind on what he should be doing. Thankfully there is a pub a few hundred yards further on where one can steady the nerves.

A great friend of mine and one of the best landscape contractors in the country specializes in making these sorts of things. His greatest folly was called the Wicker Man and stood fully 12 m (40 ft) high; built for a film but fitting equally well into any estate. His legs were Elm trees and his body wattle hurdles. Such materials, although ultimately perishable, have a life of at least 15 years and would make a fittingly eccentric addition to the landscape. Jack Sexton is a gifted man, possibly one of the last professional folly builders left in the country. He is always open to commissions and the results are spectacular.

While a faithfully reproduced greyhound does not qualify, little stone pigs or eccentric goats are certainly humorous enough to be one of a supporting cast of gnomes and other small creatures. Animals and people in bronze can also look terrific, provided they are not just straight caricatures. The great sculptor, Bernard Meadows, has produced high drama with some of these, his bronze warriors looking exceptionally menacing in long grass.

While some sculptors might disagree I always feel that a number of the larger pieces, and by that I mean over 3 m (10 ft) high, have a definitely follied feeling. This is not disparaging and both Barbara Hepworth and Henry Moore have made in no small measure contributions to the landscape and garden scene. I am sure sculptors would agree that not all of their work should be viewed without humour and the more outrageous the execution the more profound the response. It is one very sensible way of eliciting a reaction, of whatever kind, from the public. If you achieve that you have achieved a great deal and certainly increased awareness with it.

But again, this kind of sculpture makes a heavy demands on the pocket. Are there cheaper options that allow ordinary mortals a similar artistic outlet?

TOPIARY

Topiary certainly does, but not the unadventurous kind. What you need is a degree of panache. The hunting scene, with fox and hounds in full flight across a lawn is a well known and excellent example. This particular group is at the Ladew Topiary gardens in Maryland, U.S.A., although you can see several others along similar lines in England. Another astonishing display, and one that covers a huge area, lies in Tulcan, a modest town in Ecuador. Walls, arches, figures, obelisks and gateways all feature to set up an entire architectural scene in living plant material. The maintenance must be horrendous, which puts it automatically into the folly class. It looks particularly effective where it adjoins the real buildings, which are starkly white. What is more impressive is the fact that it all happens in a cemetery, the huge faces and figures taking on an ethereal quality at night.

Nearer to home the examples are splendidly idiosyncratic. A 3 m (10 ft) parrot, huge cats and dogs, horses, people, scenes of all kinds. These often dominate not only relatively small gardens but the house as well.

The best hedging plant to use is almost certainly yew, a fine evergreen that is not so slow as many people think, as long as it is fed regularly. Privet, although quick-growing, is far too rampant, needing continual clipping and with a tendency to lose its shape rapidly. Conifers of the fast growing variety are unsatisfactory for the same reasons.

If you live on chalk downland there is another possibility, provided there is ample room available. Since prehistory men have carved figures and animals in the hillsides by removing the turf and topsoil. Chalk is slow to colonize with plants and keeps its pristine appearance for a long time. While figures several hundred feet long are clearly impractical, smaller designs are not. An aquaintance

Formality is important in this arrangement of pillars, statuary and terrace, all of which focus on the dramatic and stage managed folly.

123

of mine lives under the flight path of incoming nuclear bombers. He has cut a large and very visible nuclear disarmament sign in his garden, which is over chalk. At ground level the design is not immediately recognizable as it forms a reasonably attractive series of paths and planting. From the air the symbol is obvious, a salutary reminder to those pilots who fly regular missions.

But these are somewhat tenuous follies and it is worth seeing how we can create the genuine classical article.

BUILT IN STONE

In the chapter on gazebos we looked at several reconstituted stone designs. Such firms make a vast range of items from statues to full sized temples. The design you select depends on the overall layout of the garden, the cash available and the degree of eccentricity you feel at the time.

A splendid example, if you have a long garden and wish to emphasise a vista, is an 'off-the-peg' obelisk. This stands on a 1.5 m (5 ft) square base. The top being nearly 7.2 m (24 ft) above the ground, impressive to say the least.

You can of course erect it and leave it in a pristine condition and aesthetically this is quite in order, as many of the folly builders did just that. If however you wish to 'distress' it, then take a hammer to it – carefully. Reconstituted stone crumbles a lot more easily than the real thing and although a complete ruin has its attractions it may not be exactly what you want. When you have knocked it about sufficiently give it a once over with the diluted liquid manure that we also discussed earlier. It will soon aquire a patina of age. It is perhaps an interesting thought that many original follies, built to imitate classical features from Greece or Rome, now look a lot worse for wear than the real thing. In many instances this is due to atmospheric pollution close to our large cities.

An obelisk, or 'distressed' statue is one thing but if you are really into follies then only a building will do. How about a Doric temple in severe decay with wild planting and an air of mystery? Difficult? – not a bit of it. The main prerequisite is simply care and sensitivity. Nearly anyone can build something to look good, new and true; it takes a bit more to age it a couple of hundred years.

There is available, again off-the-shelf, a superb Doric temple, circular in shape 3 m (10 ft) in diameter. It has five columns and measures, to the top of the pediment, just over 2.4 m (8 ft). The floor is paved and there is an optional domed fibreglass roof. Although not all of it will be standing, you need to purchase the entire building, apart from the roof, which is impossible to break up realistically. The base needs to be laid first, on a solid foundation of well broken hardcore, topped with rolled ash or sharp sand. The paving can then be bedded in mortar, but make sure this is slightly uneven, with one or two slabs cracked and well out of true. It is advizable to fix the slabs firmly, anything less, like a sand foundation, will be far too unstable and bring the whole temple down in a couple of weeks. Not at all the effect we are looking for!

The columns go up next, or at least three of them and one of the others can be sawn in half to cut through the reinforcing rods. The clean cut can later be distressed to remove the crisp edges. The bottom half of the column can be stood in place, the top laid on the ground as though fallen. The last column can also be sawn into several pieces which can be subsequently arranged also to appear as fallen. The lintels can be carefully positioned between the standing columns and the cornice finally positioned at the highest level. The remaining lintels and cornice will be on the ground in various disarray.

After the usual fertilizer application, we need to think about planting, and for once this is where all the traditional garden baddies can hold sway. Bramble, nettle, bindweed and dock will all look fine, together with a sprinkling of as many wild flowers as you can lay your hands on. *Don't* go and dig these up, unless you already grow them. There are a number of excellent specialist growers that supply both seed and young plants at very reasonable prices. Cracks between paving are ideal spots, crevices hacked out of stonework (an old file is invaluable) and pockets formed by several pieces of 'fallen' masonry. Planting can also frame and soften the outline, but make this as natural as possible, definitely no garish summer bedding plants here!

If you do all this, then in 18 months you will have a folly to be proud of and very little maintenance to boot. Follies can indeed be a very relaxed garden feature.

GROTTOES

The grotto is perhaps the ultimate garden folly and certainly not impossible. For those that still have a bomb shelter, this is the perfect answer to an almost impossible lump of concrete. Bomb shelters are practically impossible to move, even with power tools, and contrary to popular belief do not make good mushroom farms or wine cellars. They are nearly always decrepit and dripping with damp. Depending upon the size, the entrance may or may not need widening, and concrete steps wind their way down to various depths. The latter can be faced in stone and the inside of the shelter can also be lined completely with rock if you have the determination and the wherewithal. I have seen several shelters rebuilt in this way, complete with pools, fountains and in one case an underground hi-fi system playing suitably sombre music.

If you don't have a bomb shelter there are other avenues open, which in many ways are preferable as you can then site the grotto wherever you like in the garden. If you have a natural slope so much the better as you can build the feature into this. In a garden with rising ground you can, with a degree of hard work, create a realistic valley scene complete with interlocking spurs, the grotto being built into one of these. The feature would be above ground, the back lined with rock and a pool, complete with statue in front. Water is recirculated via a submersible pump to drip down the rock face in the traditional manner. Such a grotto is very much a focal point in the overall plan and to my mind has more to offer than something tucked away out of sight. Good exterior lighting would also be of real benefit here and very atmospheric.

Caves are more complicated, but nevertheless possible. Here again a slope, or substantial artificial hill is required. This will have to be excavated to form a bowl and a roof can be added using railway sleepers. While the walls can be lined with stone, the roof could be coated with 'Hypertufa'. This is an imitation rock that can be made easily at home. The ingredients consist of (by volume) one part sand one part cement and two parts sphagnum peat. The peat must be well moistened before use, but not wringing wet. Work it into a stiffish mix.

Layers of small mesh chicken wire should be nailed to the sleepers that form the roof and the hypertufa applied by trowel or by hand, using rubber gloves. Build the surface up in several layers. If you are dedicated and take time stalactites are not out of the question. Of course the whole feature could be built from sleepers, then wired and finally hypertufad all over.

In the final analysis it all comes down to good old fashioned eccentricity, and the folly is one feature where you can really let your imagination take flight.

But whether it be temple, tomb or grotto, plan it carefully. Site it well and let your astonished and admiring guests do the rest. Remember that you follow a splendid tradition, a tradition that is full of delight as well as humour, and remember lastly that your garden is a genuine reflection of your own personality – Good Luck!

Index

K

Kit-type pergolas, 57

L

Laburnum, 14, 72
Ladew topiary USA, 123
Lake, 99
Lattice work for pergola, 50–52
Lawns, small, 12, 45, 61
'Lee' Bucks, 120–121
Lighting for gazebos, 105
Lilac, 92
Lilium regale, 28
Lily, 15
Lily of the valley, 27
Loggia, 64
Long gardens, 10–12
Lonicera × americana, 28
　japonica
　　'Aureoreticulata', 61
　periclymenum, 97
Lutyens, Edward, 21, 50–53, 81

M

Magnolia grandiflora, 76
Malus 'Veitch's Scarlet', 101
Manholes, 24
Manuring stone paving, 99–100
Maple, 14
Measuring up gardens, 9
Metal pergola, 69
Mill folly, 117–120
Mimulus, 61
Monet's garden, 76
'Montecute' Somerset, 80
Mortar, coloured, 22
'Munstead Wood' Surrey, 81

N

Narrow gardens, 42
Nicotiana alata, 92
　'Lime Green', 15

O

Oak, 102
Obelisk, 124
Oil tank desguise, 68
'Orchards' Godalming, 52

P

Parthenocissus henryana, 27–28
Passion flower, 32
Paths, bricks, 28
　double, 61
Paved areas, for pergolas, 70
　mixed, 24
　planning, 9
　traditional materials, 12
　see also under specific materials
Pavilions, 68, 79–89, 102–103
Paviors, 61, 85–86
Pergola, circular, 13–14
　planting for, 15
Periploca graeca, 78
Philadelphus 'Belle Etoile', 27
　coronarius 'Variegata', 15
Phorium, 30
Planting designs, 14–15
Plants for arbours, 27–28
Pleaching, 20
Plymouth folly, 113
Polygonatum baldschuanicum, 75–76
　multiflorum, 27
Pools, 62
　for mill, 120
　in terraces, 35
　pergolas and, 52, 76
　walled, 91
Post sleeves, 61
Potsdam, 112
Privacy, 12
Privet, 20
Pyrus salicifolia 'Pendula', 28, 101

R

Railway sleepers for raised beds, 97
　for roofs, 125
Raised beds, 45, 75, 97
Ramblers, 76
Reeds, 99
Repton, Humphrey, 48
Rheum, 30, 86, 99
Rhododendron, 93, 120
Robinia pseudoacacia 'Frisia', 101
Robinson, William, 49
Rock garden, 97
Rogersia, 99
Roman follies, 109

garden design, 16–17
Roofs, for gazebo, 86
　railway sleeper, 125
Ropes for arches, 53
Rose, rambling, 76
　'Etoile de Hollande', 97
　'Swan Lake', 15, 28
　'Zepherine Drouhine', 22
Rosemary, 45
Rushes, 99
Rustic look, 24

S

Sackville-West, Vita, 28
St Clere, 56
Santolina incana, 24
Scale drawings, 9
Sculpture, 121
Seats, as focal points, 68
　built-in, 30
　hardwood, 22
　iron, 25
Sexton, Jack, 121
Ship's bust folly, 120–1
Shrubs, role of, 14
Sissinghurst, 28
Small gardens, 24, 29–32, 57–64
Solomon's seal, 27
Sorbus hupehensis, 101
Square gardens, 12–14
Stachys, 28
Statuary for arbours, 33
Stepping stones, 25–26, 45, 64
Steps in pergola, 53
　timber, 108
Stone blocks, reconstituted, 89
　flags, 92, 99–100, 117
　obelisk, 124
　piers for pergolas, 53–56
Stowe Castle, 113–116
　Park follies, 113
Summerhouses, 84
Sundial, 64
Swimming pools, 104

T

Temple, Doric, 124
Terraces, 13, 97
　in series, 35
Thatch for gazebo, 85, 97
'Thunder House', 81
Tile piers for pergola, 56
　roof for gazebo, 91
Timber arbours, 22, 25–27, 32, 35–41

arches, 61
boarding, 107
decking, 97, 99, 108
mill, 117–118
pergolas, 53, 56, 64, 68
preserving, 25
seats, 22
slices for paving, 25, 27
steps, 108
Topiary, 20, 123–124
Trees, 100–101
　role of, 14
Trellises, 45
　for arbours, 32–33
　for gazebo, 104
　for pergola roof, 54
Tudor garden design, 80
Tulcan garden Ecuador, 123
Tunnel, designs, 49

V

Verbascum, 45
Versailles, 110–112
Victorian garden design, 17–21, 48
Vines, 36, 68, 69, 78
　kolomikta, 69, 78
　Russian, 75–76
　silk, 78
Virginia creeper, 27–28
Vitis coignetiae, 36, 68
　riparia, 36
　vinifera, 36

W

Walls, brick, 91
　concrete block, 86
　linking role of, 24
　painted, 30
White gardens, 28
'Wickerman', 121
Widening gardens visually, 10, 24
Wilhelmshohe, 112
Willow, 101
Wires for pergolas, 76
Wisteria, 30–32, 72, 76
Witley Park follies, 116
'Woodside' Chenies, Bucks, 52
Wooton House folly, 113
Wright, Whitaker, 116

Y

Yew, training, 20, 123
Yorkstone paving, 12, 92, 117

Acknowledgements

The publishers are grateful to Macmillan Publishers Ltd (Papermac Division) for granting permission to reproduce the quotations on pp. 53 and 81, from *Gardens for Small Country Houses* by Gertrude Jekyll and Lawrence Weaver.

The publishers are also grateful to the following for granting permission for reproduction of colour photographs: Tania Midgeley (pp. 18, 55 and 110); David Stevens (pp. 19, 31, 42, 43, 75, 82, 83, 90, 107, 118 and 119); Michael Boys (pp. 34 and 58); Pamla Toler (pp. 26, 35, 59, 71, 98, 103 and 106); Jerry Harpur (pp. 11, 23, 27, 74, 94, 114 and 115); R. C. Balfour Esq. (p. 54); Tessa Traeger (pp. 63 and 66); Frank Fawkes (p. 95); and Hugh Palmer (pp. 87 and 122). The photographs on pp. 38, 47, 51 and 111 were taken by Bob Challinor.

All the line drawings were drawn by Nils Solberg. Reproduction of the drawings shown in Fig 28*a* and *b* is made courtesy of Chilstone Garden Ornaments, Sprivers Estate, Horsmonden, Kent.